LUCIA TERSIGNI & AUDREY COSSON | PHOTOGRAPHY BY EMANUELA CINO

ROME

CLASSIC RECIPES FROM THE ETERNAL CITY

MITCHELL BEAZLEY

CONTENTS

Foreword	6
A day in Rome	10

ANTIPASTI

Bruschetta al Pomodoro – Tomato bruschetta	18
Supplì al Telefono – Rice and veal croquettes with mozzarella	20
Sora Margherita	24
Fiori di Zucca Fritti– Fried courgette flowers	26
Carciofi alla Romana – Roman-style braised artichokes	31
Filetti di Baccalà Fritti – Fried salt cod fillets	32
Dar Filettaro	34

PIZZA AND BREAD

Ciriola Romana – Roman bread rolls	39
Pizza Bianca – White pizza	42
Forno Campo de' Fiori	44
Pizza Scrocchiarella – Extra crispy pizza	48

PASTA AND GNOCCHI

Bucatini all'Amatriciana – Bucatini with tomato and guanciale sauce	55
Penne all'Arrabbiata – Penne with a spicy tomato sauce	58
Gnocchi alla Romana – Roman-style gnocchi	60
Pasta alla Bruschetta – Pasta with raw tomato sauce	64
Primi	69
Fettuccine alla Papalina – Fettuccine fit for the pope	71
Pasta con le Alici – Spaghetti with anchovies	75
Paccheri alla Gricia – Pasta with guanciale and pecorino	76
Pasta e Ceci – Pasta with chickpeas	78
Tonnarelli Cacio e Pepe – Tonnarelli with cheese and black pepper	82
Spaghettoni alla Carbonara – Spaghettoni carbonara	84

MEAT AND FISH

Abbacchio a Scottadito – Grilled lamb chops — 90
Bollito alla Picchiapò – Roman-style beef stew — 95
Polpette al Sugo – Meatballs in tomato sauce — 96
Pollo ai Peperoni – Chicken stew with peppers — 100
Coda alla Vaccinara – Roman oxtail stew — 103
    Secondi — 105
Saltimbocca alla Romana – Roman-style veal escalopes — 107
Porchetta – Rolled herb-stuffed pork belly — 110
Trippa alla Romana – Roman-style tripe — 112
    Checco Er Carettiere — 114
Baccalà e Ceci – Salt cod with chickpeas — 118
Tortino di Alici e Indivia – Anchovy and curly endive 'pie' — 121

VEGETABLES

Minestra di Broccoli e Arzilla – Broccoli and skate wing soup — 124
Farricello – Cracked spelt with vegetables — 129
Carciofi alla Giudia – Jewish-style artichokes — 130
Vignarola – Braised spring vegetables — 134
Cicoria Ripassata – Sautéed puntarelle — 136
Puntarelle – Puntarelle salad with anchovy vinaigrette — 137
Zucchine alla Romana – Roman-style stuffed courgettes — 141
Broccoli e Carciofi Fritti – Romanesco broccoli and artichoke fritters — 142
Pomodori con il Riso – Tomatoes stuffed with rice — 145
Concia di Zucchine – Roman-style marinated courgettes — 146

DESSERTS

Crostata Ricotta Uvetta e Pinoli – Ricotta, raisin and pine nut tart — 152
Bignè di San Giuseppe – St Joseph's Day cream puffs — 154
Ciambelline al Vino ''Mbriachelle' – Wine biscuits — 159
Maritozzi – Brioche buns with whipped cream — 160
Crostata Ricotta e Visciole – Ricotta and sour cherry tart — 164
Tortolicchi – Almond and honey biscuits — 168
Pangiallo – The golden bread of Ancient Rome — 172
    La Merenda — 175
Grattachecca – Traditional granita — 176
    Palazzo del Freddo Giovanni Fassi — 178
Zuppa dolce alla romana – Roman sponge cake — 181
    Il Caffè — 182
    La Passeggiata — 185

Address book — 188
Index — 190
Glossary — 191
Acknowledgements — 192

FOREWORD

Traditional Roman food might be humble in appearance – and is definitely working class in origin – but it is full of treasures. It celebrates simple, everyday produce from land and sea, which is always seasonal, and which – with skilful preparation – can be transformed into unforgettable classic dishes. Roman cuisine doesn't claim to be sophisticated, but it always insists on the best quality in both ingredients and cooking, and on achieving a remarkable balance within every recipe. It celebrates mature Pecorino Romano, crispy melt-in-the-mouth guanciale (pork jowl), air-dried pancetta and, of course, homemade pasta.

This book is not about the Rome of mass tourism, with its flashy neon signs and menus translated into five languages. Instead, it is a deep dive into the Rome where the locals live, with its markets, family cooking and recipes passed down from one generation to the next. We went to meet the people who practise the old skills and knowledge of the Roman kitchen with pride, mindful of their duty to preserve what might otherwise be lost.

Rome is not exempt from the globalization which threatens gradually to erase the unique personalities of our cities. But in some Roman kitchens, *trattorie* and bars, the traditional ways are holding out. These are places where they still serve Fried Cod Fillets, *Cacio e Pepe*, Jewish-Style Artichokes, and *Maritozzi* (see pages 32, 82, 130, and 160). Places where dishes are prepared as they always have been: patiently, by hand, using fresh, seasonal produce.

Roman cuisine is built on the memories of its people. Thanks to these enthusiastic cooks and eaters, the history of the ancient city continues to be told through its dishes. The 50 recipes in this book are an invitation to bring a little bit of that traditional Rome into your kitchen, and to share it with your loved ones.

A DAY IN ROME

In Rome, meals follow an unchangeable, almost sacred, daily routine: eating is a way of life. And Rome is not short on temptations.

The morning ritual is set in stone: a strong coffee at a bar, accompanied by a soft *cornetto* pastry filled with cream, chocolate-hazelnut spread or jam. For those in a rush, a slice of *Pizza Bianca* with mortadella, folded in half like a sandwich, also does the trick (see page 42).

At lunchtime, everyone sits down for a proper meal: pasta, *supplì* rice croquettes (see page 20) or a vegetable stew. A traditional Italian meal consists of several courses: *antipasto*, *primo piatto*, *secondo piatto*, *contorno*, then *dolci*. But usually, especially at lunch, people tend to make do with one course – usually a *primo* or *secondo* with a *contorno* (vegetable dish) – reserving the full meal for Sundays or special occasions.

Coffee, drunk briskly while standing at a bar, is a feature at any time of day.

Late afternoon and it's time for *la merenda*, the sacrosanct snack for kids and peckish grown-ups. *Artisanal gelato*, *Ciambelline al Vino* dipped in fruit juice, lemonade or ice tea, or cream-filled *Maritozzi* (see pages 159 and 160). In summer, there's nothing better than a refreshing *Grattachecca* (see page 176).

Then it's time for *la passeggiata* – the evening stroll, when Romans parade around the city dressed in their finery – and the indispensable pre-dinner drinks: often a spritz with olives and cured meats... always accompanied by long, animated conversations.

Dinner is eaten late: *Fiori di Zucca Fritti*, *Pasta e Ceci*, *Saltimbocca alla Romana* (see pages 26, 78 and 107) or pizza from a wood-fired oven. Every mouthful is savoured in its own sweet time in this lively, big-hearted city that adores its food.

ANTI-PASTI

ANTIPASTI

Antipasti get a Roman meal off to a good start. They whet the appetite, pique the palate and awaken the senses. Though often small bites, they tell a big story: a tale of great bread, fruity olive oil, still-warm mozzarella, seasonal vegetables, leftover rice turned into a *crochetta*. Or, often, a perfectly golden *frittura*... fried food is an art form in Rome, a skill inherited from both peasant cuisine and Jewish traditions, which have together left a deep imprint on the city's favourite foods.

BRUSCHETTA AL POMODORO

Tomato bruschetta

This recipe transforms simple bread and tomatoes into an explosion of sunny flavours. Because there are so few ingredients, it's important to use good-quality bread and the ripest tomatoes.

- 400g (14oz) ripe round tomatoes, chopped
- 200g (7oz) ripe datterini tomatoes, finely chopped
- Extra virgin olive oil
- Small handful of oregano leaves (optional)
- 16 basil leaves, torn or sliced
- 8 slices of farmhouse loaf
- 1 garlic clove, peeled and halved
- Salt and freshly ground black pepper

Place the chopped tomatoes in a mixing bowl and season generously with olive oil, oregano (if using), salt, pepper and basil leaves. Mix and set aside to marinate for 30 minutes.

Meanwhile, toast the slices of bread in a frying pan or toaster until golden brown. Rub the garlic on the hot toast.

Spoon the tomato mixture onto the slices of bread, adding a splash of the tomato juice from the bowl for extra flavour. Serve immediately, while the toast is still crunchy.

CHEF'S TIP

Add a drizzle of balsamic vinegar, or a few curls of finely shaved Parmesan, just before serving.

SUPPLÌ AL TELEFONO

Rice and veal croquettes with mozzarella

These tasty rice balls oozing with melted mozzarella are a Roman street food classic. The name *al telefono* comes from the strings of melted mozzarella, which stretch like old-fashioned telephone cords when the supplì are cut or pulled apart.

- ½ onion, finely chopped
- Groundnut oil, for deep-frying
- 200g (7oz) minced veal
- ½ glass of white wine
- 400g (14oz) tomato passata
- 250g (9oz) carnaroli or vialone nano rice
- 500ml (18fl oz) hot vegetable stock
- 40g (1½oz) Parmesan, finely grated
- 30g (1oz) butter
- 200g (7oz) mozzarella (see tip, below)
- 3 eggs, lightly beaten
- 400g (14oz) dried breadcrumbs
- Salt

Fry the onion in a frying pan in a little of the oil for 10 minutes, until translucent. Add the minced meat and brown over a high heat for 5 minutes, turning with a spoon frequently and breaking up any clumps. Pour in the white wine and allow it to evaporate completely. Stir in the tomato passata and leave to simmer over a medium heat for around 10 minutes.

Add the rice and stir well. Gradually pour in the hot stock, 1 ladleful at a time, stirring and waiting until the liquid is absorbed before adding more.

When the rice is cooked, season with salt. Remove from the heat and stir in the grated Parmesan and butter to bind everything together. Spread the rice out on a baking tray and leave to cool completely.

Meanwhile, cut the mozzarella into 15 sticks, 3–4cm (1¼–1½in) in length.

Moisten your hands, then take a portion of the cold rice mixture, roll it into a ball and lightly flatten. Place a piece of mozzarella in the centre, close the ball tightly and roll in your hands to make a compact cylinder, completely sealing in the mozzarella.

Put the beaten eggs and breadcrumbs into 2 separate shallow dishes.

Dip each *supplì* first into the beaten eggs, then roll it carefully in the breadcrumbs, pressing slightly to make sure it is completely coated.

Heat the groundnut oil to 170°C (340°F) in a wide, deep-sided saucepan; for safety, the oil should not come more than one-third of the way up the sides of the pan and should never be left unattended. Fry the *supplì* in batches so as not to overcrowd the pan, turning them frequently, for 6–7 minutes, until golden brown.

Drain on kitchen paper and serve hot, so the mozzarella is still melted and stringy, while you repeat to cook the rest.

CHEF'S TIP

To stop the mozzarella oozing too much during cooking, use a firm cheese and leave it to drain in the refrigerator for a few hours before making the *supplì*.

SORA MARGHERITA

Nestled in the heart of the Jewish quarter, blink and you'll miss this discreetly signed trattoria, founded in 1927. The tiny dining room is always full, and deservedly so, because this is a place where the flavours of working-class Roman cuisine remain intact.

Cristina poses with her all-female team – Elena and Merian to her left, Nina and Mirella to her right – in front of the restaurant's façade, unchanged in almost a century.

Every morning, Cristina starts by hand writing the day's menu out on a sheet of paper. It features the house classics: beautifully grilled *Abbacchio a Scottadito*; melt-in-the-mouth *Polpette al Sugo*; *Coda alla Vaccinara*; and of course, *Carciofi alla Giudia*, crispy and golden brown, the mouthwatering icon of Jewish-Roman cuisine (see pages 90, 96, 103 and 130). The week's menus follow a pattern: on Thursdays it's gnocchi, Friday means fish, and every Sunday they serve a 100 per cent Roman menu.

SORA MARGHERITA
Piazza delle Cinque Scole, 30,
00186 Roma RM, Italy

When we arrived in the morning, Elena and Nina were rolling meatballs by hand. They are lightly coated with breadcrumbs before being fried.

Like many of Rome's institutions, Sora Margherita is a family affair. Cristina has run the restaurant since 2009 and, before that, it was her mother who made the fresh pasta by hand every morning. Today, Cristina still makes the seasonally inspired desserts, including the fabulous *Crostata Ricotta e Visciole* (ricotta and sour cherry tart, see page 164). Moist and fragrant, it has become one of the restaurant's classics.

This small restaurant is also about the women who work here: every morning at the crack of dawn, they are hard at work kneading, stretching and stuffing fresh pasta ready to be coated with sauces that have been simmering for hours. The copious portions are a habit inherited from the time when Sora Margherita herself used to serve the local workers. These days, the clientele may have changed but the restaurant's generosity – both in their dishes and their welcome – stays the same.

FIORI DI ZUCCA FRITTI

Fried courgette flowers

Once the first courgette flowers appear at the markets in late springtime, this irresistible Italian speciality – particularly popular in Rome – makes the perfect starter.

- 16 courgette flowers
- 180g (6oz) mozzarella
- 8 anchovy fillets
- 250g (9oz) Super fine 00 grade pasta flour
- 150ml (¼ pint) cold sparkling water
- Groundnut oil, for deep-frying
- Salt

Clean the courgette flowers and remove the stamens or pistils. Wash them, taking care not to damage them, and pat them dry with kitchen paper. Cut the mozzarella into strips (you will need 16 strips). Slice each anchovy fillet in half.

Sift the flour into a mixing bowl. Whisk in the sparkling water gradually to stop lumps forming. (See tip, below.)

In a wide, deep-sided saucepan, heat the groundnut oil to 160°C (325°F). For safety, the oil should not come more than one-third of the way up the sides of the pan and should never be left unattended.

Carefully fill a courgette flower with a piece of mozzarella and half an anchovy fillet. Close the flower by twisting the tips of petals together tightly to seal. Repeat to stuff all the flowers.

Dip each stuffed flower in the batter, then plunge it into the hot oil using tongs. Fry for around 6 minutes until golden brown. Do not overcrowd the pan; you will probably need to fry these in batches.

Drain the fried flowers on kitchen paper and lightly sprinkle with salt. Serve hot and crispy, while you fry the rest.

CHEF'S TIP

For a crunchier, lighter batter, use very cold water and add a few ice cubes just before dipping the flowers in.

CARCIOFI ALLA ROMANA

Roman-style braised artichokes

A classic Roman dish, with melt-in-the-mouth artichokes braised in olive oil, herbs and white wine.

- 4 Romanesco artichokes, or purple globe artichokes
- 1 lemon, halved
- 10 mint leaves, finely chopped
- Leaves from a bunch of flat leaf parsley, finely chopped
- 1 garlic clove, crushed
- 50g (1¾oz) fresh breadcrumbs
- 60g (2¼oz) Parmesan, finely grated
- 4 tablespoons extra virgin olive oil
- 20ml (4 teaspoons) white wine
- Salt and freshly ground black pepper

Carefully wash the artichokes, removing the toughest outer leaves down to the tender, lighter-coloured leaves. Cut off the tops of any purple leaves that remain. As you prepare the artichokes, rub the cut parts with the halved lemon to prevent browning. Peel the base of the artichokes with a sharp knife. Leave around 4cm (1½in) of stem on each artichoke, but peel it to remove the fibrous parts. Gently open the leaves and scoop out the hairy choke inside with a spoon or small knife.

Prepare the filling by mixing the chopped mint and parsley leaves in a bowl with the crushed garlic, breadcrumbs, Parmesan, salt and pepper. Fill the artichokes by placing the filling in the central hollow created from removing the chokes, as well as between the leaves.

Stand the artichokes in a deep saucepan, stems pointing upwards. Add the olive oil, 2 ladles of water and the white wine. Cover and cook over a medium heat for around 40 minutes.

Serve the artichokes hot in their cooking juices, with a little freshly ground black pepper.

CHEF'S TIP

For a bit of a kick, add a pinch of chilli flakes to the filling.

FILETTI DI BACCALÀ FRITTI

Fried salt cod fillets

Deliciously crispy on the outside and tender on the inside, these cod fillets are a perfect antipasto, but could be a main course, with side dishes. Salt cod is a traditional Roman (and southern European) delicacy, sold pre-soaked in Italian delicatessens. If yours is not ready to cook, you will need to rinse it, then soak it, changing the soaking water two or three times a day, for 24–48 hours, depending on how salty it is. (The vendor will be able to advise on its salt level.)

- 800g (1lb 12oz) salt cod, pre-soaked and ready to cook (or see recipe introduction)
- 400g (14oz) 00 flour
- 150ml (¼ pint) cold sparkling water
- Groundnut oil, for deep-frying
- Salt

Rinse the desalinated cod and dry thoroughly with kitchen paper. Remove the skin and bones if necessary. Chop into pieces of around 6cm (2½in) and chill in the refrigerator until ready to cook.

Sift the flour for the batter into a mixing bowl. Gradually whisk in the sparkling water to stop lumps forming. (See tip, page 26.)

In a wide, deep-sided saucepan, heat the groundnut oil to 170°C (340°F). For safety, the oil should not come more than one-third of the way up the sides of the pan and should never be left unattended.

Dip the pieces of cod in the batter, then drop into the hot oil in batches, so as not to overcrowd the pan. Fry for 6–7 minutes until golden brown.

Drain on kitchen paper. Sprinkle over a little salt. Serve hot and crispy, while you fry the rest.

WHERE TO EAT IT IN ROME

Dar Filettaro is a temple to fried fish fillets, tucked away in the heart of Rome's old town (see pages 34–35).

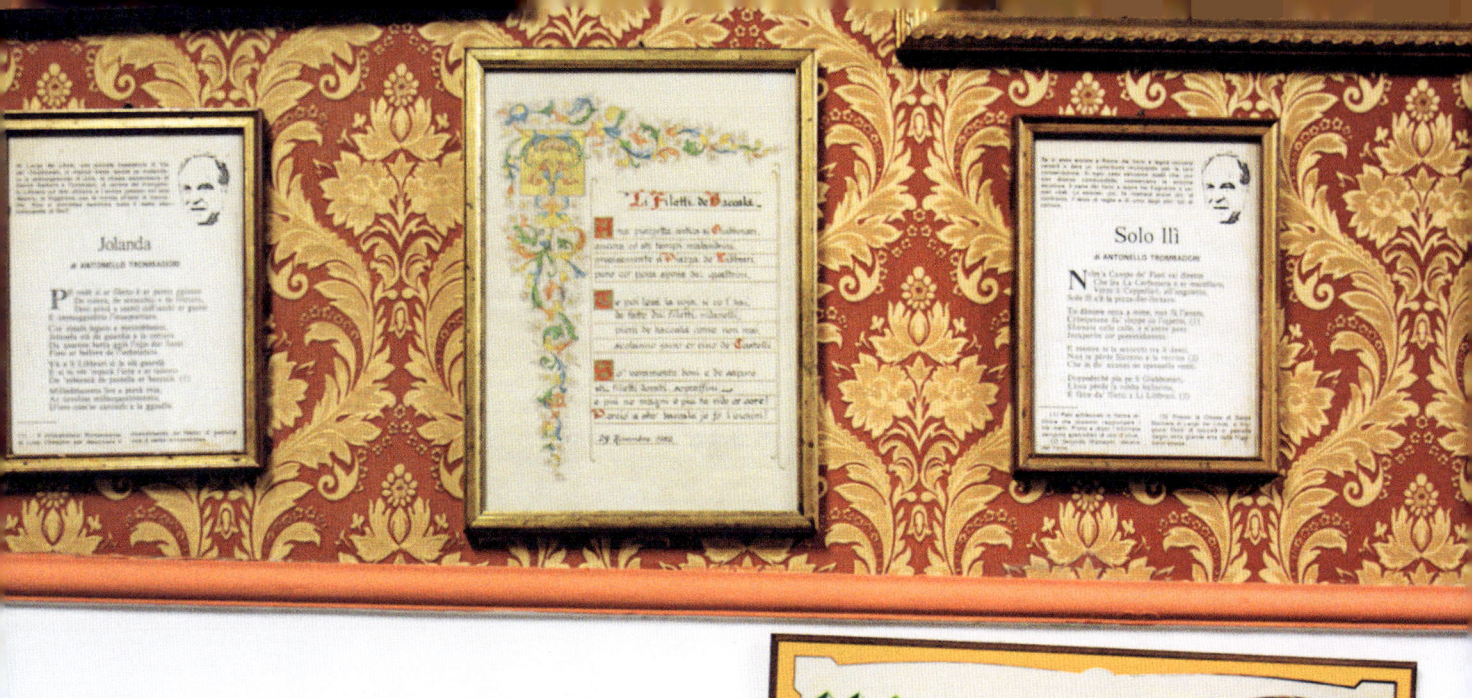

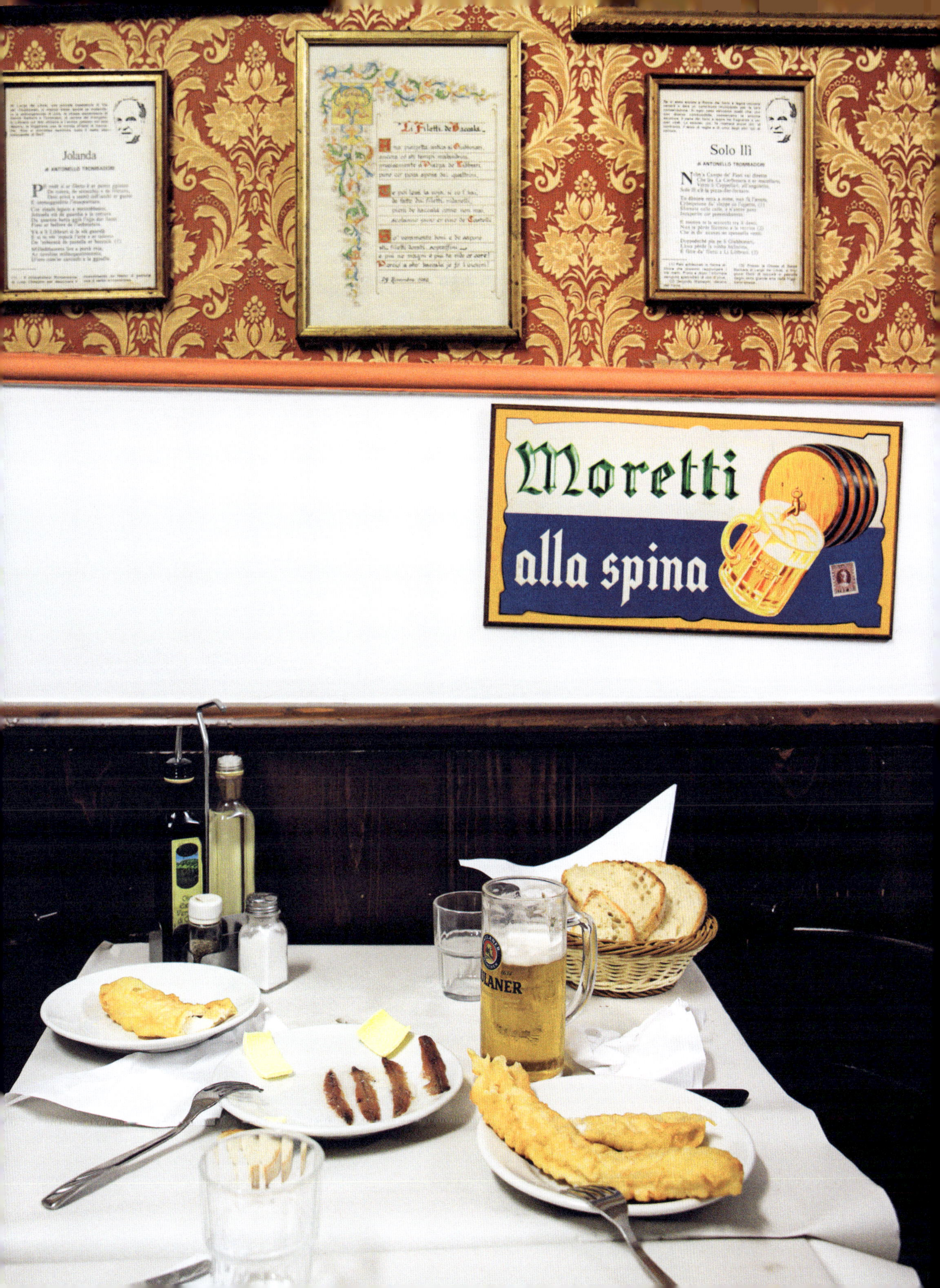
Jolanda
Solo Ilì
Moretti
alla spina

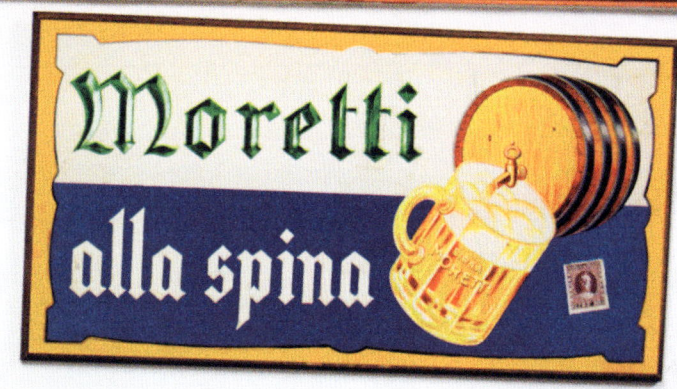

DAR FILETTARO

On a charming little square, where Santa Barbara dei Librari Church is also tucked away, a tiny restaurant serves up the best *filetti di baccalà* in Rome. Simple and ageless, it seems that time has stood still here for more than 100 years.

Every day at 5.30pm, a small sign suddenly lights up this wonderful little piazza in Rome's old town. A queue of the city's most well-informed food lovers soon forms, patiently awaiting their holy grail: a beautiful golden-brown salt cod fillet, crispy on the outside – with an audible crunch – and tender on the inside.

People mostly come here for the legendary *filetti*, but it's worth ordering the *puntarelle insalate* to accompany it, or try their delicious anchovies, prepared in-house.

It is at the back of this narrow, cosy restaurant that the magic happens. The deep fryer sizzles in the kitchen as Marcello Cortesi reveals the secret behind his fried salt cod fillets: desalinating them in water to keep them tender, double-frying for crunchiness and coating them in a tasty breadcrumb mix made with the same natural yeast that he has been using for 50 years. He took over the century-old establishment in 1978, and his daughters were practically born here. 'I ensured my legacy,' he says with a twinkle in his eye, while one daughter, Emanuela, busies herself behind the till as if she has always been there. Those waiting in the queue can rest assured that the business will continue and that the best *filetti* in Rome have plenty of crunch in them yet.

**DAR FILETTARO
A SANTA BARBARA
Largo dei Librari, 88,
00186 Roma RM, Italy**

PANE E PIZZA

PIZZA AND BREAD

Bread and pizza are an integral part of the landscape in Rome. Purchased at any time of day, they are eaten on-the-go, or carried under arms, still warm and steaming from the oven. They come in all shapes and sizes, including *Ciriola Romana*, a bread roll slit in the middle that is perfect for making panini, and *Pizza Scrocchiarella*, an extra-crispy thin pizza crust (see pages 39 and 48). Behind the apparent simplicity of the bakes lie expertise, a tasty sourdough starter and ovens that fire up before dawn. In Rome, bread isn't just an accompaniment: it is an essential.

CIRIOLA ROMANA

Roman bread rolls

Ciriola romana is found on every street corner: a delicious traditional Italian bread with a light golden crust, ideal for making tasty sandwiches.

- 250ml (9fl oz) lukewarm water
- 7g (¼oz) fresh yeast
- 10g (¼oz) honey
- 70g (2½oz) semolina flour
- 430g (15oz) 00 flour
- 10g (¼oz) salt
- Flavourless oil

Pour the lukewarm water and yeast into the bowl of a stand mixer fitted with a dough hook. Mix for a few seconds, then add the honey. Wait for the honey and yeast to dissolve, then add both the flours. Knead for 5 minutes.

Add the salt and continue to knead at medium speed for around 15 minutes to make a smooth dough. Shape the dough into a ball. Lightly brush the surface with oil to stop it drying out. Place the dough in a bowl, cover with clingfilm and slow-prove in the refrigerator for 12 hours.

Once the dough has rested, remove it from the refrigerator and leave it to stand for 1½ hours until it returns to room temperature. Tip the dough onto a work surface, and stretch into a rectangle. Fold the long sides into the centre. Repeat this 3 times, leaving the dough to rest for 15 minutes between each series of folds.

After the final rest, divide the dough into 6 pieces weighing about 120g (4¼oz) each. Shape each piece into a small sausage that tapers at each end and use a sharp knife to make a shallow slash along the top of each piece. Line a baking tray with baking parchment and place the *ciriole* on it, spacing them well apart. Cover with a clean tea towel and leave them to rise for 1 hour.

CHEF'S TIP

For an even crisper crust, place a bowl of water in the bottom of the oven while the rolls are cooking.

Preheat the oven to 220°C/200°C fan (425°F), Gas Mark 7. Once the rolls have risen, slit each lengthways down the centre with a sharp knife. Bake for 25 minutes, until the rolls are golden brown. (See tip, left.)

PIZZA BIANCA

White pizza

Pizza bianca is very popular for its crispy exterior and soft interior. Romans often eat it as a snack, wrapped around fillings, on their way to school or work.

FOR THE STARTER
- 150g (5½oz) pizza flour
- 250ml (9fl oz) water
- 2g (½ teaspoon) fresh yeast, dissolved in lukewarm water

FOR THE DOUGH
- 3g (½ teaspoon) fresh yeast, dissolved in lukewarm water
- 200g (7oz) pizza flour, plus more to dust
- 1 tablespoon extra virgin olive oil, plus more for oiling
- 5g (1 teaspoon) salt

FOR THE TOPPING
- Extra virgin olive oil
- Mortadella, finely sliced
- Pinch of sea salt flakes

First, prepare the starter. Add the 2g (½ teaspoon) yeast to the water and stir to dissolve, then mix in the flour. Cover with clingfilm and leave to ferment for 4–5 hours in a warm place, until bubbles appear.

Now for the dough. Add the 3g (½ teaspoon) of dissolved yeast to the starter, then transfer to the bowl of a stand mixer fitted with a dough hook. Knead for 10 minutes. Gradually add the flour, kneading at medium speed. Then drizzle in the olive oil while continuing to mix. Finally, add the salt. Knead for around 20 minutes to make a smooth and elastic dough. Tip the dough onto a floured work surface. Fold it twice to make a compact ball.

Place in a lightly oiled airtight container and leave to prove for 6 hours in a warm place until tripled in size.

Once it has risen, gently stretch the dough: lift one side of it up, then push it down into the centre. Repeat from the other side. Leave to rest for 10 minutes. Repeat the stretch, then leave to rest for another 30 minutes.

Preheat the oven to as hot as it will go. Oil a baking tray, place the dough on it and spread it out into a rectangle, pressing gently with your fingers. Brush with olive oil and sprinkle on sea salt flakes. Bake on the bottom shelf of the oven for 5–6 minutes. Move the baking tray up to the middle shelf and continue cooking for 8 minutes.

When it comes from the oven, split it, sprinkle on sea salt flakes and a splash of olive oil, then use to wrap mortadella like a sandwich.

CHEF'S TIP

In autumn, try making white pizza with prosciutto and seasonal fresh figs.

FORNO CAMPO DE' FIORI

Every morning, the aroma of warm sourdough bread wafts from an ancient oven across the Piazza Campo de' Fiori. Forno is more than just a bakery: it's a landmark for locals, a place they come to every day.

It is 7am. The market in Piazza Campo de' Fiori might be slowly awakening, but over at the Forno, Fabrizio's oven has been operating for hours. At midnight, the staff begin preparing the dough, which is left to rest for five or six hours, followed by another hour once it has been stretched and before it is baked. Davide has been a baker for 41 years and he tells us that the *pizza bianca* has to be ready by 8am, in time for children on their way to school and local workers off to the office or site. The 150cm- (5ft-) long, light and crusty pizza is first cut in half, then divided into portions.

FORNO CAMPO DE' FIORI
Piazza Campo de' Fiori, 22,
00186 Roma RM, Italy

The bakery sells a dozen varieties of pizza, including *bianca*, mozzarella, potato, aubergine, mushroom, cooked ham, courgette flowers and cherry tomatoes.

In the 1950s when Fabrizio's uncle returned home from Chicago, he introduced a hitherto unknown product into Italy: sandwich bread. He imported a machine from the United States and in 1962 patented his famous 'Roscioli square loaf'.

There is no 'gourmet' version here, because, as Fabrizio likes to say: 'Everyone should be able to afford pizza.' Fabrizio grew up surrounded by sacks of flour and hot crusty bread. He started work as a delivery boy at the age of 17, became a baker and eventually took over the family business. When people tell him that his pizzas are the best in Rome, he simply replies: 'There is no such thing as good wine, only the one you like best.' And it is with this modesty, and the desire to pass on his knowledge, that Fabrizio keeps this iconic bakery alive, day in, day out, guaranteeing its future.

PIZZA SCROCCHIARELLA

Extra crispy pizza

A Roman speciality with a thin, crispy crust. It is cooked quickly at a high temperature, which is what gives it such a unique crunchiness when you bite into it.

- 220g (8oz) pizza flour
- 60g (2¼oz) semolina flour
- 2g (1 teaspoon) fresh yeast, crumbled
- 150ml (¼ pint) lukewarm water
- 5g (1/8oz) salt
- 2 tablespoons extra virgin olive oil, plus more for oiling
- Sea salt flakes
- Leaves from rosemary sprigs or basil leaves (optional)

In the bowl of a stand mixer fitted with a dough hook, mix the flours with the yeast. Gradually add the measured water, kneading at medium speed to make an even dough.

Add the salt, then drizzle in the olive oil. Continue kneading until the oil is completely absorbed. Shape the dough into a ball, place in a lightly oiled airtight container and leave to prove for 7–8 hours in a warm place.

Preheat the oven to 240°C/220°C fan (475°F), Gas Mark 9.

Using a rolling pin, roll the dough out thinly on a floured surface. Place it on an oiled baking tray, brush with olive oil and sprinkle on sea salt flakes and rosemary leaves, if using.

Bake in the oven for 5–6 minutes until golden brown. Serve warm, to enjoy its fabulous crispiness.

CHEF'S TIP

Feel free to top the dough with other herbs, or ingredients of your choice, such as pitted olives or tomato and mozzarella, before baking. But don't overload it with toppings, or it will lose its crispiness.

PASTA E GNOCCHI

PASTA AND GNOCCHI

In Rome, pasta is a serious – almost sacred – business. Pasta is shaped by hand into myriad shapes and its rough texture makes it great with *Amatriciana*, *Cacio e Pepe*, or *Carbonara* sauces (see pages 55, 82, and 84), among so many others.

There is an old Roman saying relating to the city's weekly menu: *Giovedì gnocchi, Venerdì pesce, Sabato trippa*. It means that, traditionally, Romans ate tender and filling gnocchi on Thursday, fish on Friday and tripe on Saturday. Roman gnocchi are unlike those known worldwide; here, they are made with semolina flour, cut into discs and browned in the oven.

As ever in the Roman kitchen, a few simple ingredients suffice, along with a little patience and a lot of love.

BUCATINI ALL'AMATRICIANA

Bucatini with tomato and guanciale sauce

A mainstay of traditional Italian cuisine, this originated in Amatrice in the Lazio region. Bucatini – a type of long hollow pasta – literally sucks in the sauce, for a great taste experience.

- 120g (4¼oz) guanciale
- 2 tablespoons extra virgin olive oil
- 400g (14oz) can of plum tomatoes, crushed with a fork (see tip, below)
- 320g (11½oz) bucatini pasta
- 50g (1¾oz) Pecorino Romano, finely grated, plus more to serve
- Salt and freshly ground black pepper

Remove the rind from the guanciale and slice it into strips around 1cm (½in) thick. Heat the oil in a nonstick frying pan, add the guanciale and gently melt it over a low heat for around 10 minutes until the fat turns translucent. Then increase the heat and brown it for a further 5 minutes until it is crispy on the outside and soft on the inside. Remove the guanciale from the pan, leaving the fat behind, and keep warm.

In the same pan, use the fat from the guanciale to fry the crushed tomatoes. Season with a pinch of salt and ground black pepper. Cover and simmer for 30 minutes.

Meanwhile, cook the bucatini in a large saucepan of boiling water until al dente, according to the packet instructions.

Once the sauce has cooked for 30 minutes, return the guanciale, setting a few pieces aside for serving, and simmer for a few minutes over a medium heat so that the flavours combine.

Drain the bucatini, reserving its cooking water. Add the pasta to the sauce with half the pecorino and a splash of the cooking water, stirring until well coated. Cook over a medium heat for 2 minutes. Remove from the heat and stir in the rest of the pecorino. If the sauce is too thick, splash in a little more cooking water.

Serve the bucatini, scatter with the extra guanciale, sprinkle generously with pecorino and add a twist of freshly ground black pepper.

CHEF'S TIP

For an even more authentic taste, use San Marzano tomatoes, known for their sweetness and low acidity.

PENNE ALL'ARRABBIATA

Penne with a spicy tomato sauce

This simple recipe made with tomato and chilli is perfect for those who love authentic dishes with a bit of a kick.

- 400g (14oz) can of peeled plum tomatoes
- 100g (3½oz) tomato sauce, homemade or shop-bought
- Chilli flakes, or finely chopped red chilli, to taste
- 5 tablespoons extra virgin olive oil
- 1 garlic clove, peeled but left whole
- 320g (11½oz) penne rigate pasta
- Flat leaf parsley leaves, finely chopped
- Salt

Drain the canned tomatoes and tip them into a mixing bowl. Crush with a fork, then add the tomato sauce. Stir in chilli to taste.

In a frying pan, heat the olive oil with the garlic clove over a low heat for around 10 minutes, until the garlic releases its aromas (see tip below). Add the tomato and chilli pepper mixture, stir well and season with salt. Leave the sauce to simmer for 20 minutes.

Meanwhile, cook the penne in a large saucepan of salted boiling water until al dente, according to the packet instructions. Drain and tip straight into the frying pan with the sauce. Stir over a high heat for 2 minutes to coat the pasta with the sauce.

Serve the penne piping hot, scattered with parsley.

CHEF'S TIP

Be careful not to burn the garlic, as this can make the sauce bitter.

GNOCCHI ALLA ROMANA

Roman-style gnocchi

Gnocchi alla romana is a traditional speciality, made with durum wheat semolina and grilled in the oven. Their melt-in-the-mouth texture and, here, the delicate taste of sage butter, make them absolutely irresistible either on their own as a starter, or served with braised meat as a side dish.

- 1 litre (1¾ pints) whole milk
- 80g (2¾oz) butter, plus more for the tray
- Ground nutmeg
- 250g (9oz) semolina flour
- 2 egg yolks
- 80g (2¾oz) Grana Padano cheese, finely grated
- Small handful of sage leaves
- Salt

In a saucepan, bring the milk to the boil with 30g (1oz) of the butter, a pinch of salt and a pinch of ground nutmeg. When it reaches boiling point, sprinkle in the semolina flour, whisking vigorously to stop lumps forming.

Cook the mixture for around 15 minutes, until it starts to come away from the sides of the pan. Remove from the heat and stir in the egg yolks using a wooden spoon. Gradually add 40g (1½oz) of the Grana Padano, stirring well until fully mixed.

Divide the mixture in half. Spread each half on a sheet of baking parchment and roll into a log shape, using the paper to help. Place the 2 rolls in the refrigerator for around 1 hour until firm.

Preheat the oven to 200°C/180°C fan (400°F), Gas Mark 6. Remove the rolls from the refrigerator and slice them into discs around 1cm (½in) thick. Arrange the gnocchi on a buttered baking tray.

Italian comfort food: the softness of semolina and the aroma of buttered sage and cheese.

Melt the remaining 50g (1¾oz) of butter and brush it on the gnocchi, then put the sage leaves on top. Sprinkle over the remaining 40g (1½oz) Grana Padano, then bake for around 20 minutes.

Finally, place under a hot grill for 5 minutes until browned. Serve piping hot.

CHEF'S TIP

For an even crunchier, more golden-brown crust, mix a handful of breadcrumbs into the remaining Grana Padano and scatter over the gnocchi before baking. This makes for a delicious contrast between soft gnocchi and crispy topping.

PASTA ALLA BRUSCHETTA

Pasta with raw tomato sauce

This dish, served at room temperature, embodies the central philosophy behind all Italian cuisine: use few ingredients, but let them be of the best quality, and treat them simply.

- 320g (11½oz) fusilli pasta
- 5 tablespoons extra virgin olive oil
- 300g (10½oz) ripe tomatoes
- 200g (7oz) buffalo mozzarella
- 150g (5½oz) caciotta cheese (or see tip, below right)
- Finely chopped red chilli, to taste
- 10 basil leaves, torn
- Salt

Boil the fusilli in a large saucepan of salted water until al dente, according to the packet instructions. Once cooked, drain and place in a bowl, stir through the olive oil and set aside to cool.

While the pasta is cooling, finely chop the tomatoes and reserve their juice.

Add the tomatoes and tomato juice to the pasta, then tear or grate over nuggets of the mozzarella and caciotta. Season with a pinch of salt, the chilli and basil leaves. Mix well so all the ingredients are evenly distributed.

Leave the mixture to rest for around 10 minutes before serving to allow the flavours to blend.

CHEF'S TIP

If you cannot find caciotta, replace it with a young Pecorino Romano.

PRIMI

Primi piatti are an essential part of a traditional Italian meal. They can be pasta, rice or soup, and are served immediately after the antipasti and before the meat or fish. In Rome, pasta dishes often take centre stage and tend to be hearty, copious and nourishing: filling comfort food. The classic sauces include *Amatriciana*, *Cacio e Pepe*, and *Carbonara* (see pages 55, 82 and 84): all simple, straightforward and with few ingredients, yet bursting with flavour and incredibly well-balanced, born of an expertise passed down through the generations. Each one is proof that a simple pasta dish can create an unforgettable meal.

FETTUCCINE ALLA PAPALINA

Fettuccine fit for the Pope

A more delicate variation of the famous carbonara, this is a typically Roman dish made to please the sophisticated Papal palate. You will need a pasta machine to make the fettuccine. Alternatively, use 320g (11½oz) shop-bought fettuccine, and cook according to the packet instructions until al dente.

FOR THE HOMEMADE FETTUCCINE
- 200g (7oz) 00 flour, plus more to dust
- 2 whole eggs
- 1 egg yolk
- ½ tablespoon olive oil
- Pinch of coarse sea salt

FOR THE SAUCE
- 80g (2¾oz) cured ham (see tip, below)
- 30g (1oz) butter
- 30g (1oz) onion, finely chopped
- 2 egg yolks
- 120g (4¼oz) double cream
- 40g (1½oz) Parmesan, finely grated, plus more to serve
- Salt and freshly ground black pepper

CHEF'S TIP

To make this recipe according to the authentic Roman recipe, use superior quality cured ham such as San Daniele or prosciutto di Parma, and take care not to overcook the sauce, to preserve its creamy texture.

To make the pasta, tip the flour into a mixing bowl and make a well in the centre. Pour the rest of the ingredients into the well and mix, gradually knocking in flour from around the edges until it is all incorporated. Knead the dough for 10 minutes, then cover the bowl in clingfilm. Set aside to rest for 30 minutes at room temperature.

Cut the dough into 8 pieces and keep them covered while you work on one piece at a time. Flatten the first piece, sprinkle with flour and pass through a pasta machine on the thickest setting. Fold the resulting strip over itself in thirds lengthways, then pass it through the machine again on the same setting. Repeat once more, then pass through the machine on the second-thickest setting. Continue this process up to setting 7. Lay the strip on a floured surface and cover with a tea towel, then repeat with the other pieces of dough.

Using a pasta cutter or knife, slice each strip into long strips 6–8mm (¼–⅜in) wide.

Now for the sauce. Cut the ham into strips around 5mm (¼in) wide. Melt the butter in a frying pan over a low heat. Add the onion and leave to sweat for 5 minutes, adding a little lukewarm water. Once the water has evaporated, add the ham and fry for 5 minutes. Turn off the heat.

In a mixing bowl, combine the egg yolks and cream. Add the Parmesan along with a generous pinch of ground black pepper, then beat vigorously with a fork to make a smooth sauce.

Cook the fettuccine in a large saucepan of salted boiling water for 2–3 minutes. Remove from the water with a slotted spoon and drain, but reserve the cooking water.

Transfer the fettuccine to the frying pan with the ham and stir for 1 minute, adding the pasta cooking water to coat. Turn off the heat and immediately stir in the sauce, mixing quickly so it remains creamy. If the sauce is too dry, add a splash more cooking water.

Serve hot, with a sprinkling of grated Parmesan and ground black pepper.

PASTA CON LE ALICI

Spaghetti with anchovies

A delicious and simple dish of Mediterranean origin, which combines the piquancy of anchovies with the heat of garlic and chilli. If you prefer a milder taste, use whole garlic cloves and remove them after cooking.

- 16 fresh whole anchovies (or see tip, below right)
- 4 tablespoons extra virgin olive oil
- 2 garlic cloves, germ removed and finely sliced (or see recipe introduction)
- 1 red chilli, left whole
- 320g (11½oz) spaghetti pasta
- Handful of flat leaf parsley leaves, chopped
- Salt and freshly ground black pepper

Clean the fresh whole anchovies under running water, then remove their heads and backbones.

Set a nonstick frying pan over a medium heat, pour in the oil, then add the garlic and chilli. Brown over a medium heat for 7–8 minutes, then remove the chilli once the oil has absorbed its flavour.

Meanwhile, bring a large saucepan of salted water to the boil. Cook the spaghetti until three minutes short of al dente, according to the packet instructions.

Put the anchovies in the frying pan with the oil and garlic, add a ladleful of the pasta cooking water and simmer over a low heat. Three minutes before the spaghetti is cooked to al dente, drain it and transfer to the frying pan. Mix it with the anchovy sauce over the heat until well coated.

Serve the spaghetti hot, scattered with parsley and ground black pepper.

CHEF'S TIP

If you cannot find fresh anchovies, replace with anchovy fillets marinated in olive oil. You will need 32 anchovy fillets for this recipe.

PACCHERI ALLA GRICIA

Pasta with guanciale and pecorino

A recipe from the Lazio region, the name of which may either be derived from the village of Grisciano, or from *gricio*, the medieval Roman word for bakers or food merchants. This dish dates backs to a time before tomatoes first arrived in Italy.

- 160g (5¾oz) guanciale
- 2 tablespoons extra virgin olive oil
- 360g (12½oz) paccheri pasta
- 80g (2¾oz) Pecorino Romano, finely grated, plus more to serve
- Salt and freshly ground black pepper

Remove the rind from the guanciale and slice it into strips around 1cm (½in) thick. Heat the oil in a nonstick frying pan, add the guanciale and gently melt it over a low heat for around 10 minutes until the fat turns translucent. Then increase the heat and brown it for a further 5 minutes until it is crispy on the outside and soft on the inside. Remove the guanciale from the pan, leaving the fat behind, and keep warm.

Meanwhile, bring a large saucepan of salted water to the boil and cook the paccheri until they are al dente (see tip, below). Drain, reserving the cooking water, and tip into the frying pan containing the guanciale fat. Cook over a high heat, adding a ladleful of the cooking water to create an emulsion. Then return the pieces of guanciale and carry on stirring to make a creamy sauce.

Turn off the heat and stir in the grated pecorino and a splash more of the cooking water, stirring quickly to obtain a thick, creamy texture.

Serve the paccheri piping hot, with a sprinkle of pecorino and freshly ground black pepper.

CHEF'S TIP

Take care not to add too much salt to the pasta cooking water, as the cheese and guanciale both already have a high salt content. For a more intense flavour, use extra-mature Pecorino Romano.

PASTA E CECI

Pasta with chickpeas

This rustic dish is one of the many typical Italian recipes from the *cucina povera* tradition. Literally translating as 'poor kitchen', this involves transforming simple, inexpensive ingredients into tasty comfort food.

- 400g (14oz) can of chickpeas
- 5 tablespoons extra virgin olive oil, plus more to serve
- 2 garlic cloves, peeled but left whole
- 1 rosemary sprig
- Handful of sage leaves
- 200g (7oz) ditalini pasta
- Salt and freshly ground black pepper

Drain the chickpeas and rinse in a sieve under running water to remove the starchy liquid.

In a large saucepan, heat the olive oil with the whole garlic cloves, rosemary sprig and most of the sage leaves. Add the chickpeas and cook for a few minutes so that they absorb the flavours.

Pour in 500–600ml (18–20fl oz) of hot water and cook over a medium heat for 10 minutes. Then remove the garlic, rosemary and sage.

Increase the heat and bring to the boil, then add the ditalini to the pan. Cook according to the packet instructions, stirring occasionally.

Serve piping hot, with a drizzle of extra virgin olive oil, the remaining sage leaves and a pinch of freshly ground black pepper to bring out the flavours.

CHEF'S TIP

For a more colourful version, add a generous spoonful of tomato sauce (homemade or shop-bought) while cooking the chickpeas.

This pairing of grains and pulses goes back to the time of Ancient Rome: a culinary tradition steeped in history.

TONNARELLI CACIO E PEPE

Tonnarelli with cheese and black pepper

This dish dates back to the era when shepherds in the Lazio region spent long periods of time in the mountains. They took with them nourishing ingredients that kept easily: Pecorino Romano, black pepper – an affordable spice that also helped preserve food – and pasta, usually tonnarelli or spaghetti, which keep well when dry. You can also use 320g (11½oz) of shop-bought tonnarelli, if you prefer, cooking it until al dente according to the packet instructions.

FOR THE HOMEMADE TONNARELLI
- 300g (10½oz) 00 flour, plus more to dust
- 200g (7oz) semolina flour
- 5 eggs
- Salt

FOR THE SAUCE
- 5g (2½ teaspoons) Black peppercorns
- 300g (10½oz) Pecorino Romano, plus more to serve
- 100g (3½oz) Parmesan
- Extra virgin olive oil
- 2g (1 teaspoon) freshly ground black pepper

Start with the tonnarelli. On a work surface, make a pile of the two types of flour with a well in the centre. Tip the eggs into the middle and, using your hands, mix them in from the centre, gradually knocking in the flour from around the edges until it is all incorporated (around 10 minutes). Cover with clingfilm and leave to rest for 30 minutes.

Divide the dough into 4–5 portions, then roll out each portion with a rolling pin to around 4mm (¼in) thick. Leave to dry for 30 minutes.

Cut the dough into strips about 3mm (⅛in) wide. The tonnarelli should look like squared-off spaghetti strands. Place on a clean, floured tea towel.

Lightly toast the peppercorns – both types, if using – in a frying pan over a low heat, then crush coarsely with a pestle and mortar.

In a large mixing bowl, mix the pecorino, Parmesan, toasted crushed pepper, a splash of olive oil and enough cold water to make a creamy sauce.

Cook the tonnarelli in a large saucepan of salted boiling water for 8–10 minutes. Remove with a slotted spoon and place directly into the bowl with the sauce, reserving the cooking water. Beat briskly with a large fork so that the pasta is well coated without lumps. If you like, add a splash of the cooking water to obtain a creamier result.

Serve hot with an extra sprinkle of pecorino and freshly ground black pepper.

SPAGHETTONI ALLA CARBONARA

Spaghettoni carbonara

A classic of Roman cuisine, carbonara as we know it today is said to have originated in Rome after the Second World War, when American soldiers stationed in Italy used to mix their rations of powdered eggs and bacon with the local pasta. The Italians adapted this idea, using fresh egg yolks, guanciale and Pecorino Romano.

- 130g (4½oz) guanciale
- 2 tablespoons extra virgin olive oil
- 320g (11½oz) spaghettoni pasta
- 4 egg yolks
- 60g (2¼oz) Pecorino Romano, finely grated, plus more to serve
- Salt and freshly ground black pepper

Remove the rind from the guanciale and slice it into strips around 1cm (½in) thick. Heat the oil in a nonstick frying pan, add the guanciale and gently melt it over a low heat for around 10 minutes until the fat turns translucent. Then increase the heat and brown it for a further 5 minutes until it is crispy on the outside and soft on the inside. Remove the guanciale from the pan, leaving the fat behind, and keep warm.

Meanwhile, bring a large saucepan of salted water to the boil. Cook the spaghettoni until al dente, according to the packet instructions. Drain, reserving the cooking water.

In a small bowl, beat the egg yolks with the grated pecorino, a generous amount of black pepper and 1 tablespoon of the melted guanciale fat until you get a smooth sauce.

Adding cream is an absolute no-no! The creamy texture should come solely from the emulsion made with the pasta cooking liquid, egg yolks and pecorino.

Pour a ladleful of the pasta cooking water into the frying pan used for the guanciale, add the drained pasta and toss quickly off the heat. Now pour the egg yolk mixture over the pasta. Stir vigorously to coat the pasta and create the sauce. If the mixture is too dry, add a splash more of the cooking water for a creamy consistency.

Return the guanciale to the frying pan and give it a final stir. Serve the pasta piping hot, sprinkled with grated pecorino and freshly ground black pepper.

WHERE TO EAT IT IN ROME:

We were lucky enough to be able to watch Stefania in action at Checco er Carettiere restaurant (see page 114) preparing carbonara sauce. It's all in the technique: vigorous whisking, a generous sprinkling of pecorino, and a well-practised eye for creating a perfectly creamy and smooth sauce without measuring anything.

CARNE E PESCE

MEAT AND FISH

In Rome, when it comes to meat, suckling lamb (*abbacchio*) is king, whether roasted, grilled or stewed (see page 90). Beef is either stewed slowly for hours until it's pull-apart tender or shaped into polpette meatballs (see pages 95 and 96). Then there is the fish and seafood, where once again the traditional Roman dishes are simple and straightforward: pan-fried skate with or without sauce, sardines marinated in olive oil, or salt cod with chickpeas (see page 118). But at the very heart of the city's working-class food is offal: *Coda alla Vaccinara* braised with celery, and *Trippa alla Romana* with tomato and mint (see pages 103 and 112). No-frills comfort food with few ingredients, cooked to perfection.

ABBACCHIO A SCOTTADITO

Grilled lamb chops

Scottadito is an iconic Roman dish that celebrates the tenderness and delicate flavour of milk-fed lamb. Traditionally eaten at Easter, this succulent recipe pays tribute to the shepherding roots of the Lazio region. Serve with sautéed vegetables, roast potatoes or a potato salad.

- 1kg (2lb 4oz) lamb chops, ideally milk-fed suckling lamb
- 2 garlic cloves, chopped into large chunks
- 1 rosemary sprig, snipped into smaller sprigs
- 5 tablespoons extra virgin olive oil, plus more to serve
- Salt and freshly ground black pepper
- Lemon, cut into wedges

Soften the meat portion of the chops using a meat tenderizer.

Arrange the lamb chops in a large dish. Add the garlic, rosemary, salt, black pepper and extra virgin olive oil. Leave in the refrigerator to marinate for at least 2 hours.

Once the meat has marinated, heat the grill or a nonstick frying or griddle pan. Cook the chops over a high heat for 4 minutes on each side, until they are golden brown and crispy.

Add salt to taste and serve hot with a drizzle of olive oil and lemon wedges for squeezing.

FORMIEA
BESSIO
PAVIMENTI

BOLLITO ALLA PICCHIAPÒ

Roman-style beef stew

Dive into the flavours of Roman cuisine with this stewed beef, a warming dish that's full of flavour and perfect for a cold day.

- 3 onions
- 1 carrot, chopped
- 1 celery stick, chopped
- 2 cloves
- 2 bay leaves
- 1kg (2lb 4oz) beef brisket, cut into chunks
- 50ml (2fl oz) extra virgin olive oil
- 2 x 400g (14oz) cans of peeled plum tomatoes, drained, then crushed with a fork
- Chilli flakes, to taste
- 6 basil leaves
- Handful of chopped flat leaf parsley leaves
- Salt

Put 1 whole onion and the carrot, celery, cloves, bay leaves, meat and salt into a large cooking pot, then just cover with water. Bring to the boil, then reduce the heat to its lowest. Leave to simmer for around 4 hours, regularly skimming off the impurities with a slotted spoon. Once the meat is cooked, leave it to cool in the stock, then shred by hand. Strain the stock.

Finely chop the 2 remaining onions. Fry them in a frying pan with the olive oil and a ladleful of the beef stock. Sweat over a low heat for around 15 minutes.

Add the crushed tomatoes, chilli flakes, basil, shredded meat and its strained stock. Stir, cover and simmer over a low heat for around 30 minutes.

Taste and adjust the seasoning with salt. Serve piping hot, with a generous sprinkling of chopped parsley.

CHEF'S TIP

To save time, and deepen the flavours, you can braise the beef a day ahead of serving.

POLPETTE AL SUGO

Meatballs in tomato sauce

These scrumptious meatballs are cooked in a tomato sauce that's bursting with flavour. Perfect with fresh bread, pasta or polenta to mop up the sauce, this is classic Italian comfort food.

FOR THE MEATBALLS

- 120g (4¼oz) white bread, weighed without crusts
- 50g (2fl oz) milk
- 400g (14oz) minced beef
- 200g (7oz) minced veal
- 100g (3½oz) minced pork
- 1 whole egg
- 1 egg yolk
- 50g (1¾oz) Parmesan, finely grated
- 30g (1oz) Pecorino Romano, finely grated
- Handful of chopped flat leaf parsley leaves
- 0.2g (⅛ teaspoon) ground nutmeg
- 2 tablespoons extra virgin olive oil
- Freshly ground black pepper

FOR THE TOMATO SAUCE

- 2 tablespoons extra virgin olive oil
- 1 celery stick, finely chopped
- 1 carrot, finely chopped
- 1 onion, finely chopped
- 1 garlic clove, germ removed, halved
- 1 litre (1¾ pints) tomato sauce, homemade or shop-bought
- Salt

Start with the meatballs. Soak the bread in a bowl with the milk for 30 minutes, then squeeze the bread to remove the excess liquid and place in a large mixing bowl. Add the minced meats, whole egg, egg yolk, Parmesan, pecorino, parsley, nutmeg and freshly ground black pepper. Knead well to obtain a consistent mixture. Shape into balls each around 50g (1¾oz) and place on a tray. Refrigerate while you make the sauce, or for up to 24 hours.

Now for the sauce. In a saucepan, heat the olive oil and fry the celery, carrot, onion and garlic for around 10 minutes, until soft. Add the tomato sauce, a splash of water and salt. Cover and simmer for 20 minutes over a medium heat. Remove the garlic from the sauce.

These moist and fragrant meatballs simmered in tomato sauce are reminiscent of family Sundays. Serve with pasta or polenta for a more substantial meal.

Heat the 2 tablespoons of olive oil for the meatballs in a nonstick frying pan. Brown the meatballs, in batches, on all sides until crispy. Drain off most of the liquid, then drop the meatballs into the hot tomato sauce. Simmer over a low heat for around 40 minutes.

Remove from the heat and stand for 5 minutes. Serve hot with a pinch of freshly ground black pepper and some good-quality bread, pasta or polenta.

CHEF'S TIP

For a moister texture, add a little ricotta to the meatball mixture.

POLLO AI PEPERONI

Chicken stew with peppers

A colourful dish with slow-cooked tender chicken and caramelized peppers. Get your butcher to cut your chicken into pieces, if you prefer.

- 2½ tablespoons extra virgin olive oil
- 1.2kg (2lb 12oz) whole chicken, cut into pieces
- 1 litre (1¾ pints) dry white wine
- 800g (1lb 12oz) red and yellow peppers, deseeded and chopped
- 500g (1lb 2oz) ripe tomatoes, deseeded and chopped
- 2 garlic cloves, halved and the germ removed
- Leaves from 1 marjoram sprig (or ½ teaspoon dried oregano)
- Salt and freshly ground black pepper

Heat the olive oil in a large frying pan that has a lid. Add the chicken pieces and brown them on all sides. Pour in the white wine and leave to evaporate over a high heat. Then remove the chicken from the pan and set aside.

Add the halved garlic cloves to the pan and fry briefly before removing them. Put the peppers in the pan and fry for a few minutes. Return the chicken to the pan, season with salt and pepper and then add the tomatoes. Cover the pan and leave to cook over a low heat for around 1 hour. Check from time to time and add a little hot water, if needed, to stop the sauce from becoming too thick.

Towards the end of the cooking time, add the marjoram leaves or dried oregano and adjust the seasoning. Serve the chicken hot.

CHEF'S TIP

For a richer flavour, you could add a pinch of sweet paprika or a few pitted black olives during cooking.

CODA ALLA VACCINARA

Roman oxtail stew

Melt-in-the-mouth meat with a fragrant tomato, celery and herb sauce: a simple, delicious dish.

- 400g (14oz) celery
- 4 tablespoons extra virgin olive oil
- 2 onions, finely sliced
- 2 garlic cloves, peeled but left whole
- 1 rosemary sprig
- 4–5 sage leaves
- 1 bay leaf
- 3 cloves
- 10–12 black peppercorns
- 50g (1¾oz) lard
- 1.5kg (3lb 5oz) oxtail, cut into pieces
- 150ml (¼ pint) white wine
- 2kg (4lb 8oz) peeled ripe tomatoes
- 600ml (20fl oz) water
- 40g (1½oz) raisins
- 50g (1¾oz) pine nuts
- 30g (1oz) 70 per cent cocoa solids chocolate, finely chopped
- Salt

Wash and clean the celery, use a vegetable peeler to remove the strings, then chop finely.

Heat the olive oil in a frying pan. Add the onions, garlic cloves and celery. Fry gently over a low heat for around 15 minutes. Then add the rosemary, sage and bay leaves, cloves and peppercorns. Cook for a further 5 minutes.

Set a large saucepan over a low heat, add the lard and gently melt for around 10 minutes until the fat turns translucent. Once melted, increase the heat and brown the oxtail pieces on all sides. This will take around 6 minutes.

Add the white wine and leave it to evaporate over a high heat. Once the wine has evaporated, stir in the peeled tomatoes and previously cooked herbs (discard the garlic cloves). Stir and simmer for around 10 minutes. Then add the measured water. Cover the pan and cook over a low heat for around 3 hours.

When the meat is cooked, add the raisins, pine nuts and dark chocolate. Season with salt, to taste. Leave the mixture to rest in the pan for about 15 minutes.

Serve the oxtail hot, with good-quality sourdough bread.

CHEF'S TIP

For more intense flavours, make the dish a day ahead and gently reheat before serving: the aromas will have had more time to develop.

SECONDI

Secondi piatti are the main course of a classic Italian meal; the centrepiece, served after the pasta or rice. They generally feature meat or fish, or occasionally eggs. In Rome, the recipes tend to be rustic and are deeply rooted in popular tradition, such as suckling lamb, *polpette* or *saltimbocca* (see pages 90, 96 and 107). These dishes might be simple, but can take skill to make well. They are often accompanied by a *contorno*: a side dish of seasonal vegetables.

SALTIMBOCCA ALLA ROMANA

Roman-style veal escalopes

This recipe pairs veal, prosciutto and sage for a rich but subtle blend of flavours. This is a dish to impress that's ready in a jiffy!

- 400g (14oz) veal fillet, cut into 8 thin slices
- 100g (3½oz) prosciutto (you'll need 8 slices)
- 8 sage leaves
- 60g (2¼oz) 00 flour
- 60g (2¼oz) butter
- 100ml (3½fl oz) white wine
- Salt and freshly ground black pepper

Place the veal slices on a chopping board and flatten with a meat tenderizer to make them thinner. Place 1 slice of prosciutto and 1 sage leaf on each slice of veal and secure with a toothpick.

Sift the flour onto a plate and dip both sides of the veal slices in the flour, making sure they are completely covered.

Melt the butter in a nonstick frying pan over a medium heat. When the butter is hot, brown the veal slices for 2 minutes on each side.

Deglaze the frying pan with the white wine, then season to taste with salt and pepper. Cook for a few more minutes so the juices thicken slightly.

Serve the saltimbocca hot, with the cooking juices poured over.

CHEF'S TIP

For the perfect accompaniment, serve the saltimbocca with mashed potato or sautéed vegetables. For a stronger taste, use a mature prosciutto, such as San Daniele.

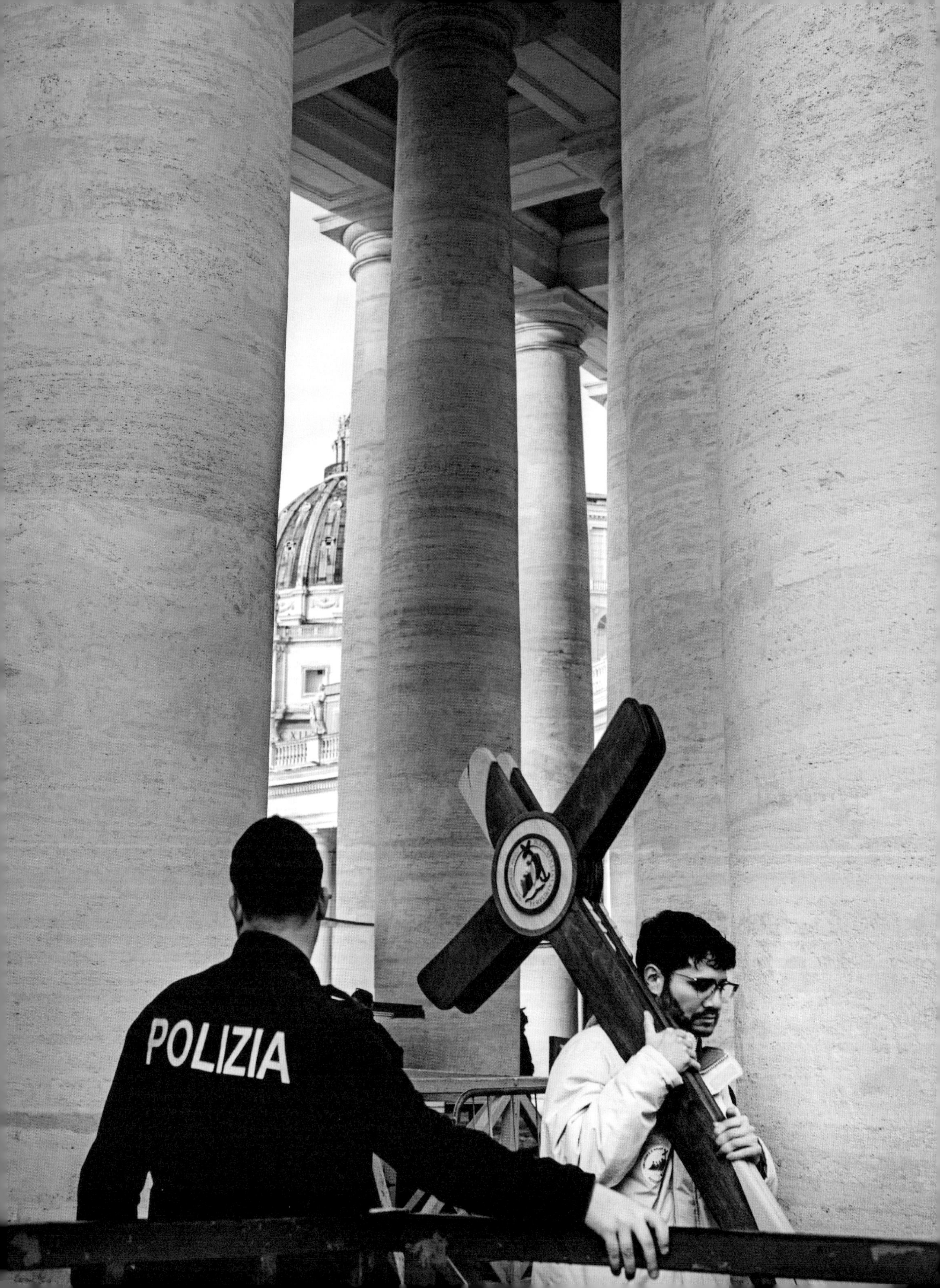
POLIZIA

PORCHETTA

Rolled herb-stuffed pork belly

A traditional dish from Lazio, which is enjoyed all over the world. This tasty, juicy roast flavoured with herbs is perfect for special occasions or indulgent family meals.

FOR THE AROMATIC OLIVE OIL

- 2 tablespoons extra virgin olive oil
- 1 garlic clove, peeled but left whole
- 1 bay leaf
- 1 rosemary sprig, plus more (optional) to serve
- 1 thyme sprig, plus more (optional) to serve

FOR THE PORK

- 2kg (4lb 8oz) boneless, skin-on pork belly
- 50g (1¾oz) fine sea salt
- 8g (¼oz) freshly ground black pepper
- 2 tablespoons white wine
- 700g (1lb 9oz) pork loin
- 15g (½oz) rosemary leaves
- 8g (¼oz) sage leaves
- 2 garlic cloves
- 20g (¾oz) fennel seeds

CHEF'S TIP

For an even more fragrant porchetta, add finely grated orange or lemon zest to the herb mixture.

Put all the ingredients for the aromatic olive oil in a small saucepan and heat gently until the oil reaches 40°C (104°F). Maintain the temperature for a few minutes. Turn off the heat, cover and leave for at least 1 hour, to let the flavours infuse.

Now for the pork: split the belly in half through its depth – so you have a piece that is half as thick and twice as wide – and open flat to form a rectangle. Sprinkle generously with the salt and pepper, then massage well so that the salt soaks in. Combine the infused aromatic olive oil with the white wine. Slather the mixture generously over the pork belly and loin in a large container. Leave to marinate for 1 hour.

Meanwhile, finely chop the rosemary, sage and garlic and roughly crush the fennel seeds. Mix well.

Preheat the oven, without the fan on, to 220°C (425°F), Gas Mark 7.

Once the pork has marinated, sprinkle the herb and fennel mix over the meat. Place the pork loin in the centre of the flesh side of the belly, roll carefully so the skin of the belly is on the outside, then tie tightly with kitchen string to make a compact roll. Make small incisions in the rind in several places.

Wrap the porchetta in foil. Place directly on an oven shelf rack, with a drip tray positioned below to collect the juices. Bake for 30 minutes until the skin starts to turn brown and harden. Remove the foil, reduce the oven temperature to 160°C (325°F), Gas Mark 3 and continue cooking for around 3 hours. Pour a little water into the drip tray occasionally, except during the last hour.

If your oven has a fan setting, turn it on during the final hour (keeping the temperature the same) for an even crispier crust but be careful not to burn the outside.

Once cooked, leave the porchetta to stand for at least 3 hours before carving. This allows the juices to permeate and ensures a great texture. Scatter with herbs, if you like, then slice and serve.

TRIPPA ALLA ROMANA

Roman-style tripe

Tripe is popular and very common in Rome. The origins of this dish date back to *cucina povera*, when the scrappiest cuts of offal were used by poorer families to make tasty, comforting dishes. These days, *trippa alla romana* still appears on menus at *trattorie* around the city, keeping the tradition alive.

- 1kg (2lb 4oz) beef tripe, cleaned and precooked
- 50ml (2fl oz) extra virgin olive oil
- 1 carrot, finely sliced
- 1 celery stick, finely sliced
- 1 onion, finely sliced
- 2 garlic cloves, halved and germs removed
- 6 mint leaves, plus more (optional) to serve
- Finely chopped red chilli, to taste
- 1.8kg (4lb) peeled ripe tomatoes, blended in a food processor
- 150g (5½oz) Pecorino Romano, finely grated
- Salt

Wash the tripe, then blanch it for 5 minutes in a large saucepan of boiling salted water. Drain, leave to cool, then cut into 1cm (½in) strips.

Heat the olive oil in a deep frying pan, then add the sliced vegetables and garlic. Fry over a medium heat for around 10 minutes, until the vegetables are soft.

Remove the garlic, then add the tripe, mint leaves and chilli and salt to taste. Fry for around 10 minutes.

Add the peeled and blended tomatoes and leave to simmer for around 30 minutes.

Serve hot with a generous handful of grated pecorino and, if you like, a few mint leaves.

CHEF'S TIP

Don't overdo the salt in this recipe, because the Pecorino Romano added at the end is very salty.

CHECCO ER CARETTIERE

At Checco er Carettiere restaurant in Trastevere, 69-year-old Stefania continues a living heritage of Roman cooking. Her grandfather – whose nickname was Checco – opened the restaurant in 1935, and the home-style food served here has been passed down through three generations of passionate cooks.

'I am not a chef, I am a *cuoche di famiglia*,' she says proudly. Literally, a 'family cook'. Along with her three sisters and her daughter, she conjures up homemade dishes following the family traditions. 'This is my home. I live here. I breathe here,' she says. 'I only use my hands. When you know what you're doing, you don't need anything else.' Stefania shows us the fettuccine that is still stretched by hand in the back kitchen. There are no gadgets here, only flour, water and a mastery of old skills.

The restaurant, located a stone's throw from the Tiber River, is an institution, a must-visit and a gathering place, where generations of customers return time and again to enjoy classic Roman dishes such as fried artichokes and spaghetti carbonara. From early in the morning, the delicious aroma of basil-infused tomato sauce fills the air in the kitchen, wafting out from a large pot that simmers gently on the stove. Every dish requires patience, knowledge and – above all – love. 'I can only cook when I feel at peace,' says Stefania, whose cooking seems fuelled by memories, aromas and emotions.

You quickly realize that this is much more than just a restaurant. It is a living bastion of popular Roman cuisine, kept alive by Checco's granddaughters, who strive every day to share the flavours of a Rome that is gradually disappearing elsewhere, but whose heart still beats here, over a low heat.

Stefania is driven both by her love for cooking and by the legacy of her father and grandfather. 'Doing something you love, that's the secret.'

CHECCO ER CARETTIERE
Via Benedetta, 10, 00153 Roma RM, Italy

BACCALÀ E CECI

Salt cod with chickpeas

A tasty, rustic dish, typical of traditional Roman cuisine for fast days, when no meat was eaten. This has wonderfully browned cod, melt-in-the-mouth chickpeas and a fragrant sauce.

- 2 garlic cloves, halved and germs removed
- 5 tablespoons extra virgin olive oil, plus more to serve
- 400g (14oz) can of tomato pulp, such as Mutti brand
- 300g cooked chickpeas, drained and rinsed weight (see tip, below right)
- 1 rosemary sprig
- 1 sage sprig
- 1kg (2lb 4oz) salt cod, pre-soaked and ready to cook (see tip, below right)
- Plain flour
- Salt and freshly ground black pepper

Fry the garlic in a saucepan with half the olive oil until they turn soft. Remove the garlic cloves, add the tomato pulp and simmer for around 10 minutes.

Add the chickpeas and season with salt, adding the rosemary and sage.

Meanwhile, chop the cod into portions, removing the skin and bones if necessary. Sprinkle flour on a wide plate and use to coat the fish, then brown in a frying pan with the remaining olive oil.

Add the cod to the tomato and chickpeas. Cook over a low heat for around 20 minutes. If the sauce gets too dry, splash in a little hot water.

Serve the cod and chickpeas piping hot, drizzled with extra virgin olive oil and scattered with a pinch of freshly ground black pepper.

CHEF'S TIPS

If using dried chickpeas, soak 100g in cold water for 12 hours, then cook for around 2 hours, or until tender, before adding to the recipe.

When buying salt cod that has not been pre-soaked, soak it in cold water for 48 hours, changing the water several times a day.

TORTINO DI ALICI E INDIVIA

Anchovy and curly endive 'pie'

This dish pairs the delicate taste of fresh anchovies with the pleasant bitterness of curly endive, or frisée. It works equally well as a starter or a light meal, and can be made in advance and served at room temperature.

- 1.2kg (2lb 12oz) curly endive (frisée)
- 5 tablespoons extra virgin olive oil, plus more for oiling
- Handful of flat leaf parsley leaves, finely chopped
- 800g (1lb 12oz) fresh whole anchovies, or 450g (1lb) fresh anchovy fillets
- 2 garlic cloves, finely chopped
- Salt and freshly ground black pepper

Preheat the oven to 180°C/160°C fan (350°F), Gas Mark 4.

Clean and wash the endive, then drain and roughly chop. Dry using a salad spinner and place in a mixing bowl. Season with salt, pepper, a drizzle of the olive oil and the parsley.

If using whole anchovies, rinse them carefully under running water and remove the heads and backbones. Rinse and gently pat dry with kitchen paper.

Oil a tart dish approximately 26cm (10 inches) wide. Lightly press the endive to remove any excess water, then spread half of it in the tart dish to make an even layer.

Arrange the anchovies on top, then scatter over the garlic and season lightly with salt.

Cover with the remaining endive, pressing down lightly to compact the layers. Drizzle with the remaining olive oil.

Bake in the oven for 30–40 minutes until lightly browned and starting to crisp at the edges.

Once cooked, leave to cool for a few minutes, before removing the tart from the dish by inverting it onto a large plate.

CHEF'S TIP

Add a few pitted black olives or capers along with the anchovies and garlic.

VERDURE

VEGETABLES

Vegetables are central to Roman cuisine and the city's colourful markets are full of them, as are the plates of its citizens, as they play a key role in daily culinary creativity. They are often cooked on their own, to bring out the natural flavours. Artichokes reign supreme here, either fried Jewish-style or braised Roman-style (see pages 130 and 134); a medley of green vegetables called *Vignarola* comes together to celebrate spring; and chicory is sautéed with garlic or served as thin crunchy shoots seasoned with anchovies (see pages 134, 136 and 137). In Rome, vegetables are not just side dishes: they are meals in their own right and speak eloquently of the culinary riches and know-how of Italy's capital city.

MINESTRA DI BROCCOLI E ARZILLA

Broccoli and skate wing soup

This traditional Roman soup has a more intense taste when served the day after it is made: prepare the skate stock ahead of time to give the flavours time to develop.

- 1kg (2lb 4oz) skate wings, cleaned
- 1 tablespoon white wine vinegar
- 80g (2¾oz) onion, cut into chunks
- 80g (2¾oz) carrot, cut into chunks
- 80g (2¾oz) celery, cut into chunks
- 5 black peppercorns
- 50ml (2fl oz) extra virgin olive oil, plus more to serve
- 1 garlic clove, crushed with the side of a blade, but left whole
- Leaves from a small bunch of flat leaf parsley, finely chopped, plus more to serve
- 2 salted anchovy fillets
- 500g (1lb 2oz) peeled ripe tomatoes, chopped
- 500g (1lb 2oz) Romanesco broccoli
- 160g (5¾oz) broken spaghetti pasta
- Salt and freshly ground black pepper

First, make the skate stock. Place the skate in a large saucepan with the vinegar, onion, carrot, celery and peppercorns, then just cover with water and salt it well. Simmer over a medium heat for around 20 minutes. Remove from the heat and leave to cool, then strain.

Once cold, shred the flesh off the skate cartilage in large pieces and set aside (discard the cartilage).

Heat the olive oil in a large frying pan. Add the garlic, fry until golden brown, then remove from the pan.

Add the parsley, anchovy fillets and tomatoes. Simmer over a medium heat for 10 minutes.

Cut the broccoli into florets and add to the frying pan. Pour over 1 ladleful of the skate stock and leave to simmer over a low heat for 10 minutes.

Add the rest of the skate stock to the frying pan, bring to the boil, then add the broken spaghetti. Cook until al dente, according to the packet instructions.

When cooked, add the reserved skate flesh and adjust the seasoning if required.

Serve piping hot, scattered with chopped parsley, a drizzle of olive oil and some freshly ground black pepper.

CHEF'S TIP

For a creamier texture, blend a small quantity of the broccoli after it has been cooking in the stock for 10 minutes, then return it to the soup.

FARRICELLO

Cracked spelt with vegetables

A dish from mountainous Central Italy whose main ingredient is *farro spezzato*, an ancient grain rich in flavour and nutrients. You can find it in some Italian delicatessens, but if you have no luck, use pearled spelt instead.

- 2 tablespoons extra virgin olive oil
- 40g (1½oz) thickly sliced pancetta, cut into strips
- 3 oregano sprigs, plus more leaves to serve
- 30g (1oz) onion, chopped
- 40g (1½oz) celery, chopped
- 40g (1½oz) carrot, chopped
- 40g (1½oz) potato, chopped
- 250g (9oz) *farro spezzato*, or cracked spelt (or see recipe introduction)
- 1–1.5 litres (1¾–2½ pints) hot vegetable stock
- Leaves from a small bunch of flat leaf parsley, finely chopped
- Salt and freshly ground black pepper

Pour the olive oil into an earthenware casserole dish or saucepan and add the pancetta. Fry over a medium heat for 10 minutes until golden brown.

Add the oregano, onion, celery, carrot and potato. Season lightly with salt and cook over a low heat for 10 minutes until the vegetables soften.

Add the spelt and pour in 1 litre (1¾ pints) of hot vegetable stock. Simmer over a low heat for 20 minutes, stirring occasionally to stop it sticking. Add more stock if needed.

Once cooked, add the parsley, a few oregano leaves and freshly ground black pepper. Mix well and serve hot.

CHEF'S TIP

For a more intense, richer flavour, replace some of the vegetable stock with chicken stock. Or serve with a drizzle of extra virgin olive oil and a sprinkle of finely grated Parmesan.

CARCIOFI ALLA GIUDIA

Jewish-style artichokes

A dish from Rome's Jewish quarter. These fried artichokes, with their crunchy leaves and tender hearts, look just like miniature suns on the plate.

- 4 Romanesco artichokes, or purple globe artichokes
- 1 lemon, halved
- 1.5 litres (2½ pints) extra virgin olive oil, for deep-frying
- Salt and freshly ground black pepper

Carefully wash the artichokes, removing the toughest outer leaves down to the tender, lighter-coloured leaves. Cut off the tops of any purple leaves that remain. As you prepare the artichokes, rub the cut parts with the halved lemon to prevent browning. Peel the base of the artichokes with a sharp knife. Leave around 3cm (1¼in) of stem on each artichoke, but peel it to remove the fibrous parts. Gently open the leaves and scoop out the hairy choke inside with a spoon or small knife.

Plunge the artichokes into a bowl of cold water and squeeze in the remaining lemon juice to prevent browning. Leave them to soak for a few minutes. Drain them and shake vigorously to remove the remaining water, then dry them thoroughly.

Gently press the leaves with your hands to slightly pull them apart, as if you were opening a flower.

WHERE TO EAT IT IN ROME

If you visit Rome's Jewish quarter, pay a visit to Sora Margherita (see page 24) just to try their wonderful fried artichokes!

In a wide deep-sided saucepan, heat the olive oil to around 150°C (300°F). For safety, the oil should not come more than one-third of the way up the sides of the pan and should never be left unattended. Drop the artichokes in and fry for around 10 minutes, turning them regularly. They should be soft but not browned.

Drain the artichokes and leave them to cool upside down on kitchen paper. (See tip, below.) Once cool, delicately open the leaves further with a fork or your fingers to make a flower shape.

Heat the oil to 170°C (340°F). Return the artichokes to the hot oil for around 2 minutes until they are well browned and crispy.

Drain them again, sprinkle with salt and pepper and serve immediately on kitchen paper.

CHEF'S TIP

For an even crunchier result, leave the artichokes to stand for an extra few minutes after you fry them for the first time, before dropping them back in the hotter oil.

VIGNAROLA

Braised spring vegetables

A dish that celebrates the arrival of spring vegetables. The name comes from the vineyards (*vigneti*) of the area around Rome, where vegetables were once grown alongside the vines. Vignarola can be served as a side dish, or used in a springtime risotto.

- 4 Romanesco artichokes, or purple globe artichokes
- 1 lemon, halved
- 50ml (2fl oz) extra virgin olive oil, plus more to serve
- 2 large spring onions, finely sliced
- 1 red chilli, finely chopped
- 200g (7oz) podded and skinned broad beans
- 200g (7oz) podded peas
- 70ml (2½fl oz) dry white wine
- 1 cos lettuce, roughly chopped
- Small handful of mint leaves
- Small handful of flat leaf parsley leaves
- Salt and freshly ground black pepper

Carefully wash the artichokes, removing the toughest outer leaves down to the tender, lighter-coloured leaves. Cut off the tops of any purple leaves that remain. As you prepare the artichokes, rub the cut parts with the halved lemon to prevent browning. Peel the base of the artichokes with a sharp knife. Leave around 3cm (1¼in) of stem on each artichoke, but peel it to remove the fibrous parts.

Cut them in quarters and remove the hairy chokes inside, rubbing with the lemon to prevent browning.

Heat the olive oil in a large frying pan, then add the spring onions and chilli. Fry over a medium heat until the onions are browned.

Stir in the artichoke quarters, broad beans and peas. Mix well, then deglaze the pan with the white wine. Leave to simmer until all the wine has evaporated.

Add the lettuce and 150ml of water. Cover and simmer over a medium heat for around 30 minutes. If the mixture becomes too dry, add a splash of hot water.

When cooked, adjust the seasoning and drizzle on some olive oil. Serve hot, scattered with mint and parsley leaves.

CHEF'S TIP

Add a few crispy guanciale or pancetta lardons at the start of cooking, for a rich, smoky flavour.

CICORIA RIPASSATA

Sautéed puntarelle

A staple side dish in Roman cuisine, this garlicky chicory sautéed with chilli and olive oil is simple, rustic and full of character.

- 1kg (2lb 4oz) puntarelle (*cicoria di catalogna*)
- 5 tablespoons extra virgin olive oil
- 2 garlic cloves, halved and germs removed
- 1 red chilli, deseeded and finely chopped, plus more (optional) to serve
- Salt

Bring a large saucepan of salted water to the boil.

Clean the puntarelle, removing any tough outer leaves and thick stalks. Carefully wash several times to remove any trace of soil.

Plunge the chicory in the boiling water and cook for 10 minutes. Drain thoroughly, reserving 1 glass of the cooking liquid.

Heat the oil in a large pan. Add the garlic and chilli and fry over a medium heat for a few minutes, then remove the garlic once it has browned.

Add the chicory to the pan, season with salt and stir. Add a splash of the cooking liquid to stop it drying out and cook for 10 minutes, stirring regularly.

Serve hot, accompanied by farmhouse bread and, if you like, a little more chopped chilli.

CHEF'S TIP

For a more intense flavour, add a few anchovy fillets to the oil, garlic and chilli at the start of the cooking process.

PUNTARELLE

Puntarelle salad with anchovy vinaigrette

In the markets of Rome, it is common to see vegetable sellers preparing heads of puntarelle by slicing them meticulously with a special tool – a *taglia puntarelle* (see page 139)– to make the characteristic thin, crunchy strips. They are then plunged into ice-cold water to curl them, before serving with an anchovy vinaigrette.

- 1.5kg (3lb 5oz) puntarelle (*cicoria di catalogna*) (or see tip, below right.)
- 2 teaspoons white wine vinegar, plus a dash for the ice-cold water
- 1 garlic clove
- 4 anchovy fillets in oil
- 1½ tablespoons extra virgin olive oil
- Salt and freshly ground black pepper

Remove the inner shoots of the heads of puntarelle. Clean them, removing any tough thick stalks. Carefully wash several times to remove any trace of soil.

Using a sharp knife, cut each shoot in half lengthways, then slice into strips that are as thin as possible. Plunge the strips into a bowl of ice-cold water with a dash of vinegar added. Leave to soak for around 1 hour. This makes the puntarelle curl and become crunchy.

Meanwhile, using a pestle and mortar, crush the garlic and anchovy fillets together to make a smooth paste. In a mixing bowl, combine the olive oil, the 2 teaspoons of vinegar, the anchovy and garlic paste, salt and pepper. Whisk vigorously to emulsify the vinaigrette.

Drain the puntarelle and carefully pat dry with a clean tea towel. Tip into a salad bowl, pour on the vinaigrette, toss and serve immediately.

CHEF'S TIP

For maximum freshness, prepare the anchovy vinaigrette in advance, to allow the flavours to emerge. Keep it in the refrigerator and take it out a few minutes before serving.

If you cannot find puntarelle, endive or chicory would work well as an alternative.

ZUCCHINE ALLA ROMANA

Roman-style stuffed courgettes

A tasty filling brings out all the flavour of steamed courgettes in this light dish.

- 6 courgettes, different colours, if you like
- 5 tablespoons extra virgin olive oil
- 1 onion, finely sliced
- Chilli flakes, to taste
- 400g (14oz) can of tomato pulp, such as Mutti brand
- 200g (7oz) minced beef
- 100g (3½oz) stale bread, blitzed into crumbs
- 2 tablespoons finely grated Parmesan
- 1 egg white
- Leaves from a small bunch of flat leaf parsley, finely chopped, plus more to serve
- Ground nutmeg
- Salt

Wash the courgettes and cut in half lengthways, then scoop out the flesh. Chop the flesh and set aside.

Heat the oil in a large nonstick frying pan over a low heat and fry the onion for 10 minutes, until soft. Add the chilli and tomato pulp, then cover and simmer over a medium heat for 10 minutes.

Meanwhile, in a mixing bowl, mix the minced meat, breadcrumbs, chopped courgette flesh, Parmesan, egg white, parsley, a pinch of nutmeg and salt. Knead the mixture with your hands to make an even filling.

Stuff the courgettes with the mixture, then place them in the frying pan with the tomato sauce. Add 1 glass of water, cover and cook over a medium heat for around 30 minutes, checking that the tomato sauce does not dry out too much (if it does, add a splash more water).

Serve the courgettes hot in the sauce, sprinkled with parsley, with fresh bread so you can mop up every last drop.

CHEF'S TIP

Feel free to add a few basil leaves to the tomato sauce. This dish tastes even better reheated the next day, when the flavours have had time to marry together.

BROCCOLI E CARCIOFI FRITTI

Romanesco broccoli and artichoke fritters

What could be more addictive than these light and fluffy vegetable fritters? And they're very easy to make, too.

- 3 Romanesco artichokes, or purple globe artichokes
- 1 lemon, halved, plus lemon quarters to serve
- 500g (1lb 2oz) Romanesco broccoli
- 400g (14oz) plain flour
- 3g (½ teaspoon) fast-action dried yeast
- 180ml (6fl oz) cold sparkling water
- Salt
- Groundnut oil, for deep-frying

CHEF'S TIP

For an even crunchier texture, replace a little of the plain flour in the batter with cornflour.

Prepare the batter by mixing the flour and yeast in a bowl and gradually whisking in the sparkling water to avoid lumps. Leave to rest in a warm place (around 24°C/75°F) for around 30 minutes.

Carefully wash the artichokes, removing the toughest outer leaves down to the tender, lighter-coloured leaves. Cut off the tops of any purple leaves that remain. As you prepare the artichokes, rub the cut parts with the halved lemon to prevent browning. Peel the base of the artichokes with a sharp knife. Leave around 3cm (1¼in) of stem on each artichoke, but peel it to remove the fibrous parts.

Cut them in quarters and remove the hairy chokes inside, rubbing with the lemon to prevent browning.

Clean, wash and break the broccoli into florets.

Bring a pan of salted water to the boil, drop in the broccoli florets and cook for 5 minutes. Drain and plunge them immediately into cold water to halt the cooking process.

Drain the artichokes, then carefully pat all the vegetables dry with a tea towel.

In a wide deep-sided saucepan, heat the oil to 160°C (325°F). For safety, the oil should not come more than one-third of the way up the sides of the pan and should never be left unattended.

Dip the vegetables in the batter, working in batches so as not to overcrowd the pan. The broccoli florets and artichoke quarters should remain separate during frying and not stick together. Fry in the hot oil for 7–8 minutes until golden brown. Pat dry on kitchen paper, sprinkle with salt and serve hot, with lemon quarters, while you fry the rest.

POMODORI CON IL RISO

Tomatoes stuffed with rice

A light dish that's simple to make, these tomatoes stuffed with rice and flavoured with basil and oregano can be eaten hot or cold, and are perfect for a summer's day.

- 12 ripe round tomatoes
- 4 tablespoons extra virgin olive oil
- 1 garlic clove
- Leaves from a bunch of basil
- 1 oregano sprig
- 12 tablespoons long-grain or basmati rice
- Salt and freshly ground black pepper

Preheat the oven to 180°C/160°C (350°F), Gas Mark 4. Line a roasting tin with baking parchment that has been dampened and any excess water shaken off.

Wash and dry the tomatoes. Slice the tops off, around two-thirds up each tomato, and scoop out the flesh carefully with a spoon, making sure not to split the skins. Put the pulp in a sieve, to drain off the juice.

Place the tomato pulp (without the juice) in a food processor with 2 tablespoons of the olive oil, the garlic, basil leaves, oregano, salt and pepper. Blend until smooth, then tip into a mixing bowl. Add the rice to the purée and mix well. Leave to rest in the refrigerator for around 1 hour, to allow the rice soak up the flavours.

Once the rice filling is ready, stuff the tomatoes with the mixture. Replace the tops of the tomatoes and arrange in the tin. Drizzle over the remaining 2 tablespoons of olive oil. Cover with foil.

Bake in the oven for around 50 minutes, removing the foil for the last 30 minutes. Allow to cool slightly before serving.

CHEF'S TIP

Add a few chopped potatoes around the tomatoes in the roasting tin. They will absorb all the juices and flavours while cooking and can be served alongside, for a more substantial meal.

CONCIA DI ZUCCHINE

Roman-style marinated courgettes

A recipe that celebrates courgettes with a fragrant, mouth-watering marinade. Serve as a side dish or an antipasto. The courgettes are fried, then marinated and traditionally eaten cold.

- 800g (1lb 12oz) courgettes, different colours, if you like
- Leaves from a bunch of flat leaf parsley, finely chopped
- Small handful of mint leaves, finely chopped
- 3 garlic cloves, halved, the germs removed
- 1 litre (1¾ pints) extra virgin olive oil, plus more for marinating
- 3 tablespoons white wine vinegar
- Salt

Wash and dry the courgettes. Cut lengthways into slices 6–7mm (¼–⅜in) thick, ideally using a mandolin to make even slices.

Place the chopped herbs and garlic in a mixing bowl, then add a splash of olive oil.

Pour the 1 litre (1¾ pints) of oil into a wide deep-sided saucepan. For safety, the oil should not come more than one-third of the way up the sides of the pan and should never be left unattended. Once it reaches 160°C (325°F), drop in the courgette slices, working in batches to avoid overcrowding the pan. Fry until golden brown, then pat dry on kitchen paper. Repeat until all the courgette slices are fried.

A typically Roman dish , passed down from generation to generation: the courgettes are fried, then marinated and traditionally eaten cold.

Arrange the fried courgette slices in a deep dish. Season with the parsley, mint, garlic and oil mixture, adding the white wine vinegar and salt.

Leave the courgettes to cool, then marinate in the refrigerator for at least 3 hours.

Remove from the refrigerator 30 minutes before serving, to allow the courgettes to come to room temperature.

CHEF'S TIP

For a version with even more flavour, add finely grated lemon or orange zest to the herb and garlic marinade. Marinate it overnight, for a more intense taste.

DOLCI

DESSERTS

The classic desserts of Rome tell stories; for Romans, they are intimately connected to childhood memories, the seasons or community celebrations. They are often connected to a specific time of year: cream puffs made for St Joseph's Day in March; sweet fruit breads at Christmas; refreshing *Grattachecca* in summer (see pages 154, 172 and 176). Many desserts are made from a combination of ricotta, dried fruit, honey or wine, with a touch of rustic indulgence typical of traditional working-class cuisine. These are unpretentious treats to enjoy at the end of a meal, with coffee, or while strolling through the streets of Rome.

CROSTATA RICOTTA UVETTA E PINOLI

Ricotta, raisin and pine nut tart

This *crostata* is particularly popular in Rome's Jewish quarter, where it is prominently displayed in the window of every bakery. Make sure you get sheep's milk ricotta for this dish, as it is such a key ingredient.

FOR THE SHORTCRUST PASTRY
- 165g (5¾oz) chilled butter, chopped into chunks
- 330g (11½oz) 00 flour, plus more to dust
- 1 whole egg
- 2 egg yolks
- Finely grated zest of 1 lemon
- 130g (4½oz) caster sugar
- Icing sugar, to serve (optional)

FOR THE FILLING
- 60g (2¼oz) raisins
- 20ml (4 teaspoons) rum
- 700g (1lb 9oz) sheep's milk ricotta
- 130g (4½oz) icing sugar
- 50g (1¾oz) pine nuts

CHEF'S TIP

Crostata tastes even better the day after it is made, as this gives the flavours time to develop.

Prepare the pastry. In a mixing bowl, or the bowl of a stand mixer fitted with the paddle or whisk attachment, blend the chunks of cold butter with the flour until you obtain a grainy mixture. Add the egg, egg yolks, lemon zest and sugar. Mix at medium speed for 2–3 minutes, until you obtain a smooth mixture. Flatten the pastry lightly with your hands, wrap in clingfilm and leave to rest in the refrigerator for at least 30 minutes.

Prepare the filling. Soak the raisins in the rum in a small bowl, adding just enough water to cover them. Strain the ricotta in a sieve to remove any excess liquid.

Put the strained ricotta in a mixing bowl, add the icing sugar and whisk until smooth and even in texture. Drain the raisins and add to the ricotta along with the pine nuts. Mix well.

Preheat the oven to 180°C/160°C fan (350°F), Gas Mark 4.

Turn the rested pastry out onto a lightly floured surface and knead briefly to make it more elastic. Divide into 2 parts, one slightly larger than the other (the larger portion is for the base). Roll out the pastry for the base to around 1cm (½in) thick. Line a 28cm (11in) diameter tart tin with baking parchment, then place the pastry for the base in the tin.

Pour the ricotta filling onto the pastry and smooth it out in an even layer.

Put the smaller half of the pastry between 2 sheets of baking parchment and roll out to 5mm (¼in) thick. Cut it into strips approximately 2cm (¾in) wide and arrange them on top of the filling in a lattice pattern.

Bake in the oven for around 45 minutes, until the *crostata* is lightly browned, leaving it for longer if the pastry does not seem cooked or browned enough. Cool completely before removing from the tin. Dust with icing sugar, if you like, before serving.

BIGNÈ DI SAN GIUSEPPE

St Joseph's Day cream puffs

Bignè di San Giuseppe are a traditional Italian speciality, made to celebrate St Joseph's Day on 19 March.

FOR THE CUSTARD CREAM

- 1 litre (1¾ pints) whole milk
- Pared zest of 1 lemon, removed with a vegetable peeler
- 1 vanilla pod, split lengthways and seeds scraped out
- 6 egg yolks
- 200g (7oz) caster sugar
- 45g (1¾oz) 00 flour
- 45g (1¾oz) cornflour

FOR THE BIGNÈ

- 120ml (4fl oz) water
- 10g (¼oz) sugar
- 60g (2¼oz) butter
- 90g (3¼oz) 00 flour
- 2 whole eggs
- Salt

TO SERVE

- 12 canned or fresh Amarena cherries
- Icing sugar, to dust (optional)

Start with the custard cream. Heat the milk in a saucepan with the lemon zest strips and vanilla seeds and pod to boiling point. Remove from the heat.

In a separate saucepan, whisk the egg yolks and sugar together. Gradually add the flour and cornflour, whisking to avoid lumps.

Strain the hot milk to remove the zest and vanilla pod, then gradually add it to the egg mixture, whisking all the time.

Return the pan to a medium heat and cook, stirring constantly, until the cream thickens. Once thickened, continue cooking for 5 minutes, then remove from the heat. Pour into a heatproof bowl, cover with clingfilm so it is touching the surface (to prevent a skin from forming) and leave to cool completely.

Now make the bignè. Preheat the oven to 220°C/200°C fan (425°F), Gas Mark 7 and line a large baking tray with baking parchment.

In a saucepan, heat the measured water with a pinch of salt, the sugar and butter until it comes to the boil. Remove from the heat and tip all the flour in. Mix vigorously with a spatula. Return the saucepan to a low heat and continue stirring for 3 minutes, until the mixture comes away from the sides of the saucepan.

Transfer the dough to a bowl and leave to cool. Then add the eggs one at a time, mixing the first in well to fully incorporate before adding the next.

Put the dough into a piping bag fitted with a 1.5cm (⅝in) nozzle. On the lined baking tray, pipe 3 concentric rings to form a mound, 5cm (2in) in diameter, spaced 4cm (1½in) apart. Repeat until you have 12 mounds.

Bake in the oven for 10 minutes, then reduce the temperature to 190°C/170°C fan (375°F), Gas Mark 5 and continue cooking for a further 12 minutes. Switch off the oven, leaving the bignè inside with the door half-open for 2–3 minutes.

Remove from the oven and leave to cool completely on a wire rack. Using a piping bag, fill the cooled bignè with the custard cream, either through a small hole in the bases, or by slicing them in half.

If you slice them in half, decorate with a cherry before closing them. Otherwise, place a small dollop of the cream on top of each bignè and pop a cherry on top. Dust with icing sugar, if you like, and serve.

CHEF'S TIP

Bignè can also be deep-fried for a more traditional version. In this case, they are not filled with custard cream.

CIAMBELLINE AL VINO ''MBRIACHELLE'

Wine biscuits

Ciambelline al Vino are typical rustic biscuits from the Roman countryside, often called *''Mbriachelle'*. This word comes from *ubriacare*, meaning 'to get drunk', because they are made using wine, and often dipped in wine, too, when eaten.

- 500g (1lb 2oz) 00 flour
- 150g (5½oz) caster sugar, plus 60g (2¼oz) for decoration
- 150ml (¼ pint) white wine
- 150ml (¼ pint) sunflower oil
- 10g (¼oz) baking powder
- 60g (2¼oz) demerara sugar
- Salt

Preheat the oven to 180°C/160°C fan (350°F), Gas Mark 4.

In the bowl of a stand mixer fitted with the paddle attachment, mix the flour, 150g (5½oz) of sugar, the wine, oil, baking powder and a pinch of salt until you have an evenly mixed, smooth dough. Wrap in clingfilm and leave to rest for about 10 minutes.

Take a piece of dough weighing around 28g (1oz) and shape into a 20cm (8in) long sausage on a work surface. Stick the ends together and seal to form a ring. Continue to form rings with the remaining dough.

Mix the 60g (2¼oz) each of caster and demerara sugars on a plate. Dip one side of each biscuit in the sugar. Arrange the sugared rings on a baking tray lined with baking parchment.

Bake in the oven for around 25 minutes until lightly browned. Leave to cool before serving.

CHEF'S TIP

To vary the flavours, you can replace the white wine with red wine, Vin Santo or Marsala. It is also traditional, in some parts of Lazio, to add aniseed to the dough.

MARITOZZI

Brioche buns with whipped cream

Maritozzi are small Roman brioche buns filled with whipped cream. Their name comes from the word *marito* ('husband'), because, in the past, fiancés gave them as love tokens.

FOR THE STARTER
- 100ml (3½fl oz) lukewarm water
- 2g (½ teaspoon) fresh yeast
- 100g (3½oz) 00 flour

FOR THE DOUGH
- 400g (14oz) 00 flour
- 5g (⅛oz) fresh yeast, crumbled
- 60g (2¼oz) sugar
- 10g (¼oz) honey, ideally acacia honey
- 175ml (6fl oz) whole milk
- 125g (4½oz) whole eggs (about 2 large ones)
- Finely grated zest of 1 orange
- 1 vanilla pod, split lengthways and seeds scraped out
- 8g (¼oz) fine salt
- 110g (4oz) butter at room temperature, roughly chopped
- Flavourless oil, for oiling

To make the starter, in a mixing bowl, mix the lukewarm water and yeast until dissolved. Add the flour and combine. Wrap in clingfilm and leave to prove for 1 hour in a warm place.

Now for the dough. In the bowl of a stand mixer fitted with the dough hook, combine the flour, crumbled yeast, sugar, honey and milk. Knead for 5 minutes on medium speed. Add the eggs one at a time and continue kneading for 10 minutes. Stir in the orange zest, vanilla seeds and salt. Add the starter and knead for a further 15 minutes. Gradually mix in the chunks of butter until completely absorbed.

Shape the dough into a ball, place in a lightly oiled bowl, cover in clingfilm and leave to rise for 2 hours in a warm place. Then refrigerate overnight.

The next day, remove the dough from the refrigerator and leave it at room temperature for 1 hour.

FOR THE GLAZE
- 1 egg yolk
- 50ml (2fl oz) milk

FOR THE FILLING
- 400g (14oz) double cream
- Icing sugar, to dust

Preheat the oven to 180°C/160°C (350°F), Gas Mark 4. Divide the dough into 80g (3oz) portions – you should get 12 – shape into oval balls, like rugby balls, and arrange on a baking tray lined with baking parchment. Cover with clingfilm and leave to rise for a further hour in a warm place. Mix together the egg yolk and milk in a small bowl and use to glaze the buns. Bake in the oven for 15 minutes.

Turn out on a wire rack to cool.

Whip the double cream until stiff. (See tip, below.) Slit each *maritozzo*, fill with the whipped cream using a piping bag and smooth the top with a spatula. Dust with icing sugar and serve.

CHEF'S TIP

To ensure the cream is firm, place the cream, bowl and whisk in the refrigerator for at least 30 minutes before whisking.

CROSTATA RICOTTA E VISCIOLE

Ricotta and sour cherry tart

This is another traditional tart from Roman Jewish cuisine, appreciated for the subtle contrast between the creamy sweetness of the ricotta and the acidity of the sour cherries.

FOR THE SHORTCRUST PASTRY
- 165g (5¾oz) chilled butter, chopped into chunks
- 330g (11½oz) 00 flour
- 2 egg yolks
- 1 whole egg
- Finely grated zest of 1 lemon
- 130g (4½oz) caster sugar
- Icing sugar, to serve (optional)

FOR THE FILLING
- 700g (1lb 9oz) cow's milk ricotta
- 130g (4½oz) icing sugar
- 350g (12oz) sour cherry jam, such as Morello

WHERE TO EAT IT IN ROME

The *crostata* made by Cristina's mother at Sora Margherita (see page 24) is one of Rome's best.

Prepare the pastry. In a mixing bowl, or the bowl of a stand mixer fitted with the paddle or whisk attachment, blend the chunks of cold butter with the flour until you obtain a grainy mixture. Add the egg, egg yolks, lemon zest and sugar. Mix at medium speed for 2–3 minutes, until you obtain a smooth mixture. Flatten the pastry lightly with your hands, wrap in clingfilm and leave to rest in the refrigerator for at least 30 minutes.

Preheat the oven to 180°C/160°C (350°F), Gas Mark 4.

For the filling, drain the ricotta in a sieve, then tip into a mixing bowl. Add the icing sugar and whisk into a smooth cream.

Turn the rested pastry out onto a lightly floured surface and knead briefly to make it more elastic. Divide into 2 parts, one slightly larger than the other (the larger portion is for the base). Roll out the pastry for the base to around 1cm (½in) thick. Line a 28cm (11in) diameter tart tin with baking parchment, then place the pastry for the base in the tin.

Spread the cherry jam over the pastry, then cover with the ricotta mixture.

Put the smaller half of the pastry between 2 sheets of baking parchment and roll out to 5mm (¼in) thick. Use it to cover the ricotta filling, then seal the edges of the pastry base and top together.

Bake for around 45 minutes.

Leave to cool, then dust with icing sugar, if you like, and serve.

TORTOLICCHI

Almond and honey biscuits

These rustic almond biscuits, with anise and citrus zest flavours and an intense honey and orange zest fragrance, are traditionally made in central Italy.

- 2 whole eggs
- 100g (3½oz) caster sugar
- 400g (14oz) whole almonds
- Finely grated zest of 3 oranges
- 15g (½oz) aniseed
- 300g (10½oz) honey
- 500g (1lb 2oz) 00 flour, plus more to dust
- 1 egg yolk, lightly beaten
- Salt and freshly ground black pepper

In the bowl of a stand mixer fitted with a paddle attachment, whisk the 2 whole eggs and the sugar on medium speed for 10 minutes. Add the almonds, a pinch of salt and pepper, orange zest and aniseed. Mix on low speed to combine well.

In a small saucepan, heat the honey to around 30°C (86°F). Drizzle into the almond mixture while beating on medium speed. Fold in the flour gradually until you obtain an even dough. Turn the dough out onto a floured surface and finish kneading by hand.

Preheat the oven to 180°C/160°C fan (350°F), Gas Mark 4 and line a baking tray with baking parchment.

Take pieces of dough weighing about 300g (10½oz) each. Make them into 35cm- (14in-) long sausages, each 3cm (1¼in) wide and 1.5cm (⅝in) thick. Place them on the prepared baking tray and brush with the egg yolk.

Bake in the oven for around 35 minutes, until golden brown.

Leave to cool for 10 minutes, then cut diagonally.

CHEF'S TIP

These biscuits keep very well in an airtight tin. They are delicious dipped in sweet wine or strong coffee, to bring out the flavours.

PANGIALLO

The golden bread of Ancient Rome

Pangiallo, literally 'yellow bread', is a Roman speciality that dates back to antiquity. Traditionally prepared at the winter solstice as a lucky charm to bring prosperity and light in the new year, it is a small, sweet bread made with dried fruit, honey, citrus fruit and nuts. Yellow saffron glaze gives the bread its characteristic bright appearance, which symbolizes the return of the sun. You will need a ready-made bread dough for this recipe.

FOR THE DOUGH
- 80g (2¾oz) raisins
- 50g (1¾oz) dried figs, roughly chopped
- 50g (1¾oz) pine nuts
- 80g (2¾oz) walnuts, roughly chopped
- 80g (2¾oz) whole almonds, roughly chopped
- 80g (2¾oz) hazelnuts, roughly chopped
- 30g (1oz) candied orange peel
- Zest of 1 orange, cut into thin strips
- 110g (4oz) ready-made bread dough
- 120g (4¼oz) honey
- 110g (4oz) 00 flour

FOR THE YELLOW GLAZE
- 2 tablespoons 00 flour
- 1 tablespoon honey, ideally wildflower honey
- 1 teaspoon extra virgin olive oil
- Pinch of saffron threads
- 2 tablespoons lukewarm water

For the dough, soak the raisins in a bowl of cold water for 20 minutes. Drain the raisins and mix them with the dried figs, nuts, candied orange peel and orange zest in a large mixing bowl, then work them into the bread dough.

Warm the honey to make it more liquid, then stir it into the mixture. Mix with a spoon to make a sticky dough. Gradually add the flour until the dough is thick but still malleable. Cover with a tea towel and leave to rest at room temperature for 1 hour.

Preheat the oven to 160°C/140°C fan (325°F), Gas Mark 3, and line a baking tray with baking parchment. Moisten your hands, divide the dough into 2 equal parts and make 2 compact round loaves. Place on the lined baking tray.

Now make the glaze in a small saucepan. Mix the flour, honey, olive oil and saffron and dissolve them in the lukewarm water. Set over a low heat, stirring continuously until you obtain a smooth and sticky paste. Brush the mixture generously onto the surface of the 2 loaves.

Bake the *pangialli* in the oven for 35 minutes, until the glaze is dry and golden. Leave to cool on the baking tray before slicing and serving.

CHEF'S TIP

These loaves can be kept for a few days in an airtight container, where the flavours will develop. They go well with a glass of sweet wine, such as Passito or Vin Santo, or with a cup of tea or coffee for a cosy afternoon snack.

LA MERENDA

Merenda is another Roman ritual. It is a small afternoon snack for children as they come running out of school swinging their rucksacks, or an afternoon treat for grown-ups. In Rome, people take their time over it: a slice of cake, a cream-filled *Maritozzo*, a freshly shaved *Grattachecca* or a few *biscotti* dipped in fruit juice or coffee (see pages 160 and 176). *Merenda* is not to be rushed; it is a peaceful and joyful moment which, for Romans, is bound up closely with childhood memories. The custom bridges the gap between lunch and dinner, and offers a brief respite from the city's frenzy.

GRATTACHECCA

Traditional granita

A refreshing Roman speciality, similar to Sicilian *granita* but with a coarser texture. Its name comes from the verb *grattare* ('to scratch' or 'to grate'), which refers to the way the ice was once shaved by hand to obtain large uneven crystals. In Rome, it has been served in street kiosks for more than a century, especially in summer, and comes in a variety of fruit syrup flavours. During summer, a refreshing watermelon version with chunks of the fruit is especially popular in the city.

- Ice (either cubes or blocks of ice)
- Amarena cherry syrup
- Fresh cherries (optional)
- Handful of mint leaves (optional)

Remove the ice from the freezer. Crush using a sturdy blender, pulse-blending so the crystals are thick and irregular in size.

Fill tall glasses with the crushed ice.

Slowly pour in the Amarena cherry syrup, allowing the liquid to seep between the crystals. Stir briskly with a spoon to distribute the flavours evenly.

Pop a few fresh cherries on top and decorate with mint leaves to add a touch of freshness, if you like.

Serve immediately with a straw and a spoon.

CHEF'S TIP

You can vary the flavours by replacing the Amarena cherry syrup with lemon, blood orange or mint syrup, or even with fresh fruit juices.

PALAZZO DEL FREDDO GIOVANNI FASSI

If Italy is the nation of *gelato*, then Palazzo del Freddo is undoubtedly its capital. If you find yourself near Rome's Termini Station in the Esquilino district, visiting this gelateria is a must at any time of year.

It all began five generations ago, when Andrea's great-grandfather, Giacomo Fassi, left his native Piedmont to move to Rome. There, he opened a shop where he sold beer and *granita*, that refreshing combination of crushed ice and fruit. His son Giovanni, then the pastry chef and ice-cream maker to the royal house of Italy, took over the business and began selling *gelato*, too, in the summer.

Andrea has a degree in political science and inherited a passion for *gelato*. While continuing the family business, he also founded a creative writing school, because he believes that creating a new flavour of *gelato* and composing an imaginative story have much in common: they are both flights of fancy!

Seeing how enthusiastic the locals were about *gelato*, Giovanni had a brainwave: in 1928, he established the first shop in Rome dedicated exclusively to selling ice cream all year round. That's how Palazzo del Freddo, often considered to be Rome's first ice-cream parlour, came into being.

The secret behind its success is that the business has always been committed to offering a luxury, artisanal product made with high-quality ingredients, but at a price that is affordable for everyone. As a result, this magnificent palazzo with its adjoining laboratory is busy summer and winter alike.

Every day, regulars flock to buy specialities such as Crema Romana, a creamy *gelato* made with ricotta and pine nuts, as well as pistachio, rice and *gianduja* – chocolate and hazelnut – in tribute to Giacomo's origins in Turin. Having chosen the flavour, generously sized scoops are popped into handmade cones, which have been dipped in melted chocolate and rolled in crushed hazelnuts, adding crunchiness and flavour to every bite.

At Fassi's, it is summer all year round.

**PALAZZO DEL FREDDO
GIOVANNI FASSI**
**Via Principe Eugenio, 65-67,
00185 Roma RM, Italy**

ZUPPA DOLCE ALLA ROMANA

Roman sponge cake

This age-old dessert is typically Roman and is often served on special occasions and for festive meals. Despite its name, it is not a 'soup' but an indulgent layered cake where the *pan di spagna* (light-as-air fat-free sponge cake) is soaked in a spiced liqueur called Alchermes, filled with a custard cream and topped with Italian meringue.

FOR THE CAKE
- 4 whole eggs
- 120g (4¼oz) caster sugar
- 120g (4¼oz) 00 flour, sifted

FOR THE CUSTARD CREAM
- 600ml (20fl oz) whole milk
- Pared zest of 1 lemon, removed with a vegetable peeler
- 5 egg yolks
- 140g (5oz) caster sugar
- 35g (1¼oz) cornflour
- 20g (¾oz) rice flour

FOR THE SYRUP
- 120ml (4fl oz) water
- 60g (2¼oz) sugar
- 150ml (¼ pint) Alchermes liqueur

FOR THE ITALIAN MERINGUE
- 50ml (2fl oz) water
- 200g (7oz) caster sugar
- 100g (3½oz) egg whites (from about 3 eggs)
- Canned or fresh cherries, to decorate

CHEF'S TIP

For a sweeter version, replace the Alchermes liqueur with rum or a red fruit syrup.

To make the sponge, preheat the oven to 170°C/150°C fan (340°F), Gas Mark 3½, and line a 20cm (8in) cake tin with baking parchment. Beat the eggs and sugar in the bowl of a stand mixer fitted with a whisk attachment for 20 minutes, until the mixture turns near-white and doubles in volume. Gradually fold in the sifted flour with a spatula. Pour into the lined tin. Bake for 20–25 minutes, leave to cool completely, then remove from the tin.

For the custard cream, bring the milk and pared lemon zest to the boil in a saucepan. Remove from the heat and leave to infuse for 20 minutes. Beat the yolks with the sugar, then sift in the cornflour and rice flour. Pour in the strained infused milk, beating continuously, then return to the saucepan over a low heat. Stir continuously until the custard thickens, then cook for a further 5 minutes. Pour into a heatproof bowl, cover with clingfilm so it is touching the surface (to prevent a skin from forming) and leave to cool completely.

Now prepare the syrup. Heat the measured water and sugar until dissolved. Remove from the heat, add the Alchermes and leave to cool.

Slice the sponge cake horizontally into 3. Brush a little syrup over the base layer, then spoon on half the custard cream. Repeat for the middle layer. Finish by adding the final layer and lightly soaking it with the syrup.

To make the Italian meringue, heat the measured water and sugar to 120°C (248°F). Meanwhile, start to whisk the egg whites in the bowl of a stand mixer fitted with a whisk attachment. Drizzle the syrup over the egg whites, whisking at high speed until you obtain a stiff, shiny meringue. Spoon into a piping bag.

Pipe the meringue all over the cake, then chill in the refrigerator for 3 hours. For a spectacular effect, you can flambé the meringue with a blow torch. Decorate with the cherries and serve.

IL CAFFÈ

In Rome, coffee is a daily essential. It is served strong and short, drunk standing at a bar – piping hot and often in one gulp – and is always delicious. For a more gentle awakening, there is cappuccino with its beautiful fine layer of foam, but beware of the unwritten Italian rule: no cappuccino after 11am. Every bar has its own character; every local their own favourite drink. When you order, you ask for a *caffè*, never for an espresso. The size of the cup encapsulates both the restless Roman temperament and the city's art of savouring the multitude of small, delicious moments in every day.

LA PASSEGGIATA

In Rome, a day rarely ends without a *passeggiata*. In summer, this is when the city gently awakens after the torpor of the afternoon, especially on the very hottest days. An evening stroll, slow and usually with no particular destination in mind, it is as much social ritual as it is a simple pleasure. People wander the narrow streets, linger on the piazzas, meet friends, then stop for a slice of pizza, a glass of wine or a plate of *antipasti*. It's a breathing space as the day comes to an end and the evening begins, when people take time to be together and nibble on something, standing at the bar or sitting on a terrace. The *passeggiata* is Rome gradually coming to life before dinnertime.

ADDRESS BOOK

Checco er Carettiere

A Roman family cuisine since 1939 and now run by Stefania and her sisters, this is a must-visit for total immersion in the working-class traditions of Trastevere.

Via Benedetta, 10, 00153 Roma RM, Italy

checcoercarettiere.it

Cucina di Casa

In a small alley near Campo de' Fiori, Rosina offers simple, generous family cuisine served in a friendly atmosphere. The perfect place for an authentic home-cooked lunch.

Vicolo delle Grotte, 27, 00186 Roma RM, Italy

rosinacucinadicasa.com

Da Etta

Located on the charming Piazza in Piscinula in the Trastevere district, Da Etta is a food emporium that is open all day and combines the charm of the past with a touch of contemporary creativity. The restaurant serves traditional Italian cuisine with a twist. It sells artisanal pastries and offers an impressive selection of more than 2000 wines, all in a friendly and welcoming atmosphere.

Piazza in Piscinula, 42-47, 00153 Roma RM, Italy

dbs-restaurants.com

Dar Filettaro a Santa Barbara

The best fried cod fillet in Rome, in a small square hidden away in the Old Town. A crunchy classic that's not to be missed.

Largo dei Librari, 88, 00186 Roma RM, Italy

facebook.com/filettidibaccala

Forno Campo de' Fiori

Iconic bakery known for its pizza bianca and wide variety of breads, a vital part of everyday life in Rome.

Piazza Campo de' Fiori, 22, 00186 Roma RM, Italy

fornocampodefiori.com

Palazzo del Freddo Giovanni Fassi

Historic ice cream parlour founded in 1928, famous for its homemade recipes and original flavours. A palace to gelato, open all year round.

Via Principe Eugenio, 65-67, 00185 Roma RM, Italy

palazzodelfreddo.it

Sora Margherita

A rustic *trattoria* in the heart of the Jewish quarter, founded in 1927. Homemade pasta, Jewish-style artichokes and a welcoming Roman atmosphere.

Piazza delle Cinque Scole, 30, 00186 Roma RM, Italy

soramargherita.com

INDEX

A

almonds 168, 172
anchovies 26, 75, 122, 137
   anchovy and endive 'pie' 125
artichokes 134
   broccoli and artichoke fritters 142
   Jewish-style artichokes 130–1
   Roman-style braised artichokes 31

B

bakeries 44–5
basil 19, 64, 95, 145
beef
   meatballs in tomato sauce 96
   Roman-style beef stew 95
   Roman-style stuffed courgettes 141
biscuits 159, 168
bread 18, 172
bread rolls 39
brioche buns with whipped cream 160–1
broccoli
   broccoli and artichoke fritters 142
   broccoli and skate wing soup 122

C

cherries 154, 176, 181
chicken stew with peppers 100
chickpeas 78, 118
chicory 136, 137
chocolate 103
coffee 181
courgettes
   fried courgette flowers 26
   Roman-style marinated courgettes
     146–7
   Roman-style stuffed courgettes 141

E

eggs 71, 84

F

figs 172
fish 32, 75, 118, 121, 124, 137
fettucine 71
filleti di baccalà 32, 34

G

gnocchi Roman-style 60
Grana Padano cheese 60
granita 175
guanciale 55, 84, 103

H

ham 71, 107
hazelnuts 172
honey 160–1, 168, 172

J

Jewish-style artichokes 130–1

L

lamb chops 90
lettuce 134

M

meatballs in tomato sauce 96
mortadella 42
mozzarella 20, 26, 64

O

oranges 168, 172
oxtail stew 103

P

Parmesan 71, 82, 96–7, 141
pasta 58
   bucatini 55
   with chickpeas 78
   fettucine 71
   with raw tomato sauce 64
   spaghetti with anchovies 75
   spaghettoni carbonara 84–5
   tonnarelli 82
peas 134
pecorino cheese 82, 84, 112
peppers 100
pine nuts 103, 152, 172
pizza 42, 48
pork 96
   rolled herb-stuffed pork belly 110
puntarelle 136, 137

R

raisins 103, 152, 172
restaurants 24–5, 34–5, 114–15, 131, 164
rice and veal croquettes with mozzarella 20
ricotta, raisin and pine nut tart 152
ricotta and sour cherry tart 164

S

sage 60, 103, 107, 110
St Joseph's Day cream puffs 154
salt cod 32, 118
spaghetti with anchovies 75
spelt 129
sponge cake, Roman 181
spring vegetables, braised 134

T

tart, ricotta and sour cherry 164
tomato pulp 118, 141
tomato sauce 96–7
tomatoes, canned 55, 58, 95
tomatoes, fresh
   chicken stew with peppers 100
   pasta with raw tomato sauce 64
   Roman-style tripe 112
   tomato bruschetta 18
   tomatoes stuffed with rice 145
tripe, Roman-style 112

V

veal
   meatballs in tomato sauce 96
   rice and veal croquettes with
     mozzarella 20
   Roman-style veal escalopes 107

W

walnuts 172
wine biscuits 159

GLOSSARY OF UK/US TERMS

INGREDIENTS

aubergine – eggplant
bicarbonate of soda – baking soda
broad beans – fava beans
caster sugar – superfine sugar
chickpea flour – gram flour or besan
chickpeas – garbanzo beans
cornflour – cornstarch
courgette – zucchini
double cream – heavy cream
golden syrup – substitute corn syrup
icing sugar – confectioners' sugar
minced beef/lamb/ – ground beef/lamb/
pork/veal   pork/veal
pepper (red/green/yellow) – bell pepper
pine nuts – pine kernels
plain flour – all-purpose flour
stock – broth

EQUIPMENT

baking paper – parchment paper
baking tin – baking pan
cake tin – cake pan
clingfilm – plastic wrap
frying pan – skillet
grill – broiler
kitchen paper – paper towels
sieve – fine-mesh strainer
tea towel – dish towel
work surface – countertop

Thank you to Aurélie for trusting in us and for her sensitive eye, which gave us the freedom to express ourselves fully.

Thank you to Chloé for her inspired staging of our work.

Thank you to Elena for her time, advice and willingness to listen – and for her unforgettable courgette flower fritters.

Thank you to Lucia, with whom working was such a natural pleasure, and whose recipes were a treat to make.

Thank you to Emanuela, with whom going on an adventure is always such fun: this book is yet another chapter in our shared memories.

Thank you to Matteo for helping me discover the city of his childhood and live life as real Romans do for a few days.

Finally, thank you to my family and to Christian for being there, for their support and for enthusiastically eating their way through every single recipe in this book.

Audrey

I would like to thank Elena who always has good thoughts to share.

I would like to thank Emanuela and Audrey who trusted me to do what needed to be done.

Lucia

Thank you, Elena, for living in such a beautiful city. It is 30 years since you moved to Rome and I started to discover it with you. It is poetic, romantic, steeped in history and extraordinary cuisine. We always love your recommendations, those hidden gems that only Romans know about. You know all its secrets, its flaws, its charms.

Thank you for the interest you have shown in our project and the help you have given us.

Thank you, Audrey, because with you I'm never afraid to share a project or an idea. I know you'll be there, 'living the moment' with simplicity, dynamism, dedication and, of course, plenty of humour.

Thank you, Lucia, for the succulent recipes you gave us. 10 out of 10!

Thank you, Aurélie, for your involvement. You always have that little extra inspiration that takes the initial idea to the next level. It is a real pleasure to work with you.

Thank you, Chloé, for your beautiful mock-up. Thank you for listening so carefully to our thoughts and feelings.

And thank you to all the wonderful people we met: Cristina and the team at Sora Margherita, Marcello Cortesi, Fabrizio Roscioli, Stefania Porcelli, Andrea Fassi. Without you there would be no authenticity in this book.

THANK YOU.

Emanuela

Originally published in France as *Rome: Les recettes authentiques et adresses secretes des Romains* by Éditions Mango in 2025.
57, rue Gaston Tessier,
75019 Paris
www.mangoeditions.com

First published in Great Britain in 2026 by Mitchell Beazley, an imprint of Octopus Publishing Group Ltd
Carmelite House
50 Victoria Embankment
London EC4Y 0DZ
www.octopusbooks.co.uk

An Hachette UK Company
www.hachette.co.uk

The authorized representative in the EEA is Hachette Ireland, 8 Castlecourt Centre, Dublin 15, D15 XTP3, Ireland
(email: info@hbgi.ie)

Copyright for original French edition © Mango 2025

Copyright for this English edition © Octopus Publishing Group Ltd 2026

Distributed in the US by Hachette Book Group, 1290 Avenue of the Americas, 4th and 5th Floors, New York, NY 10104

Distributed in Canada by Canadian Manda Group, 664 Annette St., Toronto, Ontario, Canada M6S 2C8

ISBN: 978-1-84601-730-8
eISBN: 978-1-84601-731-5

A CIP catalogue record for this book is available from the British Library.

Printed and bound in China.

10 9 8 7 6 5 4 3 2 1

English edition 2026
Commissioning Editor: Jeannie Stanley
Creative Director: Jonathan Christie
Editor: Rosie Hilton
Translation from the French: Andrea Reece
Designer: Jeremy Tilston
Senior Production Manager: Pete Hunt

All photographs by Emanuela Cino.

MIX
Paper | Supporting responsible forestry
FSC® C008047